| DATE | | | |
|------|------|------|------|
|      |      |      |      |
|      |      |      |      |
|      |      |      |      |
|      |      |      |      |
|      |      |      |      |
|      |      |      |      |
|      |      |      |      |
|      |      |      |      |
|      |      |      |      |
|      |      |      |      |
|      |      |      |      |
|      |      |      |      |

# THE ART OF
# GROWING OLD

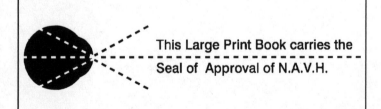

This Large Print Book carries the
Seal of Approval of N.A.V.H.

# THE ART OF GROWING OLD

## AGING WITH GRACE

---

## MARIE DE HENNEZEL

**THORNDIKE PRESS**

*A part of Gale, Cengage Learning*

GALE
CENGAGE Learning·

Detroit • New York • San Francisco • New Haven, Conn • Waterville, Maine • London

Originally published in French in France as *La chaleur du coeur empeche nos corps de rouiller; viellir sans etre vieux* by Editions Robert Laffont, 2008.
Thorndike Press® Large Print Health, Home & Learning.
The text of this Large Print edition is unabridged.
Other aspects of the book may vary from the original edition.
Set in 16 pt. Plantin.

**LIBRARY OF CONGRESS CATALOGING-IN-PUBLICATION DATA**

Hennezel, Marie de, 1946–
  [Chaleur du coeur empeche nos corps de rouiller. English]
  The art of growing old : aging with grace / by Marie de Hennezel ; translated by Sue Dyson. — Large print ed.
    p. cm.
  "Originally published in French in France as La chaleur du coeur empeche nos corps de rouiller : viellir sans etre vieux by Editions Robert Laffont, 2008."
   ISBN-13: 978-1-4104-4902-3 (hbk.)
   ISBN-10: 1-4104-4902-5 (hbk.)
  1. Aging—Psychological aspects. 2. Aging. 3. Older people—Psychology. I. Title.
BF724.55.A35H46 2012b
155.67'19—dc23
                             2012011426

Published in 2012 by arrangement with Viking, a member of Penguin Group (USA) Inc.

Printed in the United States of America
1 2 3 4 5 6 7 16 15 14 13 12

To my grandchildren:
Léa, Marie, Blanche, Gabriel,
Léonard, Céleste,
and those to come . . .

To my mother

# CONTENTS

If the only thing I had to say was that all is lost, I would keep my mouth shut.

— Jean-Louis Chrétien

The cruelest kind of growing old is not organic: it is the growing old of hearts.

— Christiane Singer

# FOREWORD

In my work as a therapist and a counselor, as well as in the hundreds of conversations I've had around the world since publishing this book, I've found, to no one's surprise, that there is nothing older than not wanting to grow old. This is as true at home in France, where sixty-eight-year-old Catherine Deneuve is still considered a sex symbol, as it is in the United States. Our world presents us with a disastrous image of old age. Women and men everywhere fear dying badly, of ending their lives alone, unloved, perhaps dependent or suffering from dementia, in lifeless places, far from everything.

Instead of confronting this fear, we ward it off by clinging to our youth in a rather pathetic state of denial. In so doing, we run the risk of missing out on what I call here "the work of growing old" — that is to say, cultivating a positive awareness of aging.

I embarked on writing this book in order to set the record straight about the reality of aging, in France and everywhere else. I read documents and listened to accounts that discouraged me. But as my research progressed, I became aware of an exciting new understanding of age, guided by some exemplary characters to whom I'll introduce you. They convinced me that the worst is not inevitable. The keys to a fulfilling old age do exist, and it's up to our generation to discover them and pass them on. It's up to us, the baby boomers, to invent a new art of growing old — which is a paradox, as it means accepting the inevitability of aging without becoming "old."

How are we to become the bearers of good tidings rather than poisonous ones to those around us? I propose that our exploration be guided by the belief that something within us does not grow old. I shall call it the heart. I don't mean the organ, which does of course age, but the capacity to love and to desire. The heart I refer to is that inexplicable, incomprehensible force that keeps the human being alive, and which Spinoza christened *conatus:* primordial energy or vital endeavor.

It is this heart that can help us push on

through our fears, and bear us up amid the worst ordeals of old age.

# I WRITE FOR MY GENERATION

Abbé Pierre, a well-known French priest who dedicated his life to helping the poor and the destitute, has just died.[1] I queue up for an hour in the Rue Saint-Jacques to bow my head before his coffin, laid out in the Val-de-Grâce chapel. An immense photograph hangs on the hospital gates, showing passersby a face that overwhelms them, a face that emanates both profound torment and an immense tenderness.

Abbé Pierre used to say that we must always keep both eyes open: one eye on the world's suffering so that we can fight against it, and the other on its wondrous beauty so that we may give thanks for it.

I have just devoted two years to writing about the experience of growing old, and throughout this exploration of the aging process I have attempted to keep both eyes open: one on all the inevitable pain, which frightens us so much, and the other on the joys that are in store for us. In order to do so, I have attempted to distance myself from the negativity, from the ambient pessimism, which foresees only bad experiences at this stage of life, and at the same time I have tried to avoid slipping into euphoria and embracing the myth of an idyllic old age.

Obtaining a balance has not been easy, for our society has a discouraging view of old age. The words *decline, horror,* and *affliction,* which spring to our lips, speak volumes about the disgust and fear that the sufferings of aging and death inspire in us.

We could leave it be, not discuss it, allow ourselves to forget about it, think about something else. That is what senior citizens do when they refuse to grow old and try to remain pathetically young and active for as long as possible.

Or, on the other hand, we can tackle old age with humor — even deride it.

Personally, as I kept one eye open to all the evils that threaten us, I began my own long descent into hell. The catastrophic image we have of old age is contagious, and I began to understand why my generation would rather close its eyes, why people change the subject as soon as I ask them what they imagine their later years will be like. In fact, I was so downcast that I almost abandoned my plan to write about such a depressing subject.

And then, one day, something inside me rejected this disastrous portrayal; something in me suddenly decided to react. You could say that the other eye, the one that appreciates the positive side of life, suddenly opened.

Thus, this book is the story of a turnaround. I had to go to the heart of the suffering and fear that the experience of growing old generates in order to understand everything it has to offer in terms of human and spiritual enrichment.

## The Island of Long Life, and the Warmth of the Heart

This journey began four years ago, when I led an evening discussion at the Place de l'Étoile in Paris devoted to the question: How should we accept growing old?[2] While I was preparing for this discussion, I discovered the island of Okinawa and its centenarians. There, in Japan, on the island that the World Health Organization has nicknamed the "Island of Long Life," people live to a great age — the oldest is 115. They are very happy, for they are regarded as good-luck charms.

Not surprisingly, researchers from all over

the world have tried to discover their secret. We know that it is not genetic, because as soon as inhabitants of the island emigrate elsewhere and begin to live in a different way, their life expectancy is reduced.

There are certainly credible links to the mild climate and dietary habits. The people of Okinawa eat little and slowly, savoring each mouthful and stopping before they feel too full. They consume fish, soybeans, algae (rich in iron and calcium), the inevitable rice, and green tea (rich in diuretics); they never eat sweet foods or pastries.

But the contents of their dinner plates do not explain everything. The extraordinary longevity of these island people, like their happiness in old age, is also linked to a cultural state of mind and a well-developed social life. These centenarians have an enhanced spiritual consciousness, which is nurtured by practices such as prayer, meditation, and focusing on the present moment, and by a determination to remain positive and optimistic in difficult times. They have that precious ability that we might term resilience: an ability not to let themselves be demoralized. Vitality, dynamism, and emotional energy — these are the keys to their inner youth, celebrated in the song they sing every morning: "The Warmth of the Heart

Prevents Your Body from Rusting."[3]

They also continue to participate in the life of the community, enjoying conversations every day with friends, neighbors, and family members. The *yuimaru,* or spirit of mutual cooperation, is very deeply rooted in their culture, and they do their gardening, their shopping, and their Tai Chi together. In short, they are happy to live to be old, and this happiness quite clearly protects them from any feeling of exclusion. They do not think that they represent a burden on society — quite the reverse. In Okinawa, people say: *"Tusui ya takara"* (The elderly are our treasure).

Why can't we, too, be good-luck charms to those around us? That is the question I asked the audience of nine hundred people who had come to hear us talk about old age.

People of our generation know that they are going to live for a long time — that's a promise. Some of us have every chance of making it to one hundred. But is this increased longevity good or bad news? That is the question that people around me are asking. We are told that this is a "golden age" for senior citizens, and some people have no hesitation in persuading us that we are the first generation to benefit from a whole new slice of life. If we take care of our health and are responsible in our diet, if we play sports and keep our minds active, then when we reach eighty we will be in the same mental and physical shape our parents were in when they were only sixty. We will have gained twenty years! Specialist literature even declares that with the decoding of the human genome, gene therapy, and the potential for nanotechnology (which will create robots so small that they can clean even the inside of our cells), we will soon be capable of permanently reconstructing a healthy, nondegradable, almost immortal body. It is a veritable revolution.

And yet we do not find this offer of a longer, healthier life reassuring. It is possible to imagine the body's cells being replaced and renewed, but things are rather more complicated when it comes to neurons and their connections. What is the good of a longer life if it means eternal dementia? Moreover, what would be the demographic impact of this progress? It has been calculated that in the global population, by 2050 there will be three people aged over sixty for every child aged four and younger.[4] How sad! If death were to be indefinitely postponed, all our benchmarks would be turned upside down. We would no longer be obliged to procreate, and we would have no further need of spiritual transcendence, as it is death's boundary that incites us to reproduce and to develop our spirituality. Death gives us the ability to imagine an existence beyond the self. Life without death would be hell!

Nevertheless, it is true that science currently offers us a real chance to extend our lives, as it is now capable of combating the "rust" that threatens our bodies. What are we going to do with this extra time, all the while knowing that we cannot escape either extreme old age or death?

This is an adventure for which we have been chosen, for we are the first generation to undertake it. As we have no points of reference, we shall have to make them up as we go along.

That is why I felt motivated to write this book. I decided that its starting point would be this question: Why shouldn't we be inspired by the example of Okinawa?

I set to work collecting personal accounts and reading a great deal about the difficulties posed by the aging population. And when I met some radiant elderly people who helped me to see old age in a different way, I realized that their radiance was very much the fruit of deliberate, clear-headed work.

One cannot lay claim to a serene, luminous old age without bidding farewell to one's youth and meditating upon one's impending death.

Dear reader, you are perhaps one of those people who prefer not to think about such things. That is understandable. You're quite happy to get older, as long as you can remain youthful. As you suspect, however, there is the unavoidable risk that you will fall prey to ageism, that you will swell the ranks of those senior citizens whom young people detest because they find them arrogant and selfish. And then the day will come when some specific event will make you topple over into true old age. On that day, you will step onto the banks of old age with terror, realizing that you will never again recapture your youth. You will face a one-way, inevitable decline. One day, perhaps, you will become completely dependent on others for survival.

This inevitable decline is well illustrated by an anecdote told to me by the French author Antoine Audouard, the former director of a large publishing house, who is often a partner to me in my writing projects.

While visiting his father, the writer Yvan Audouard, who was living out his last days as a patient in the palliative-care center of the Maison Médicale Jeanne Garnier, Antoine brought up the subject of my book. Yvan was lying down, his eyes closed, weak but very alert. When Antoine mentioned the song sung by the old people of Okinawa, "The Warmth of the Heart Prevents Your Body from Rusting," Yvan opened one eye and retorted mischievously: "Yes, but it doesn't remove the rust that's already there!"

And he was right: aging is a merciless ordeal. But this anecdote also shows that even on the threshold of death, the man who spoke these apparently pessimistic words was capable of humor and distance.

If you are not prepared for growing old, if you have not developed the necessary inner resources for getting through this last stage of life, you risk going through hell. It is possible, however, to remain happy throughout life without denying the aging process. Perhaps you are ready to confront the challenges of old age, to compensate for its inevitable losses by developing an inner life, by exploring emotional youthfulness, which can grant a certain radiance to the elderly that is obvious to those around them. If so, then this book is for you.

The pages that follow are a meditation on the art of growing old. It is a paradoxical art, for from one point of view, old age is a shipwreck; from another, it is a time of growth. From the outset, I would like to make a distinction between "growing old" and "being old." Being old is a state of mind. It is possible to feel old at sixty, and it has happened to me. It is possible to feel young at eighty. My friend, the philosopher Bertrand Vergely, recently said while attending a workshop on old age: "A person becomes old the day he becomes sad and bitter about life." We become old when we refuse to age — that is to say, when we refuse to move forward in life. This is a great paradox.

Our society forbids us to grow old, commanding us to remain young for as long as possible. This stupid prohibition contrasts with another, much more interesting one: "It is forbidden to be old," says the Hassidic mystic Rabbi Nachman of Braslaw. Grow older, but do not *be* old; that is to say, do not be bitter and despairing. Do not oppose reality, but do not prevent life from fulfilling its potential to bring forth new things, right up to your very last breath.

I am convinced that the period of time, however long it is, that separates us from old age is a chance we have been given to learn how to age, to "work at growing old," to prepare ourselves psychologically and spiritually for this final stage in our lives.

How can we accept the transformations that make our bodies ugly if we do not at the same time explore the power of emotions such as joy or gratitude? How can we accept these things if we do not stop looking at ourselves, and instead see the world around us and marvel at it? How can we accept loneliness if we have not learned to be at ease with ourselves, at peace, reconciled with our lives and with those around us?

How can we accept the constraints of limited time and space if we have not explored the limitless nature of our minds and our hearts?

Louis-Vincent Thomas wrote in his preface to my first book, *L'amour ultime* (The Final Love), that only through love, faith, and humor can we confront and perhaps transform the terrible realities of old age, decrepitude, and death. So I have chosen to don the spectacles of love, faith, and sometimes humor in order to examine the experience of growing old.

I know that in making this choice I am going against the prevailing views on old age. These views are somber and sad, and the media do not look kindly upon attempts to change them. Attempts to challenge these ideas are not well received, and anyone who wishes to display deliberate optimism is liable to face ridicule. In talking about love and faith, we run the risk of falling into the trap of edifying, moralizing, soothing language. The inane, comforting images of a happy, serene old age are for other people — don't insult us with fairy tales! Yet, on the other hand, if we acknowledge only the dark shadows of old age, the horrors of growing old and the shipwreck that awaits us, we also end up lying. The reality is not as bleak as that; it is always and everywhere a mixture of the best and the worst.

Old age is neither a complete disaster nor a golden age. It is an age that is just as rich and as worthy of being lived as all the others — an age that is exciting to live, with its joys and its difficulties. Of course, it poses problems at economic, social, and psychological levels, but we should look these straight in the eye and have the courage to anticipate them. We must find the means to light the way down our own personal path toward old age. If we try, we can discover the promises of this age, and tap into hitherto unsuspected resources that will enable us to live courageously and simply.

It is obvious that the way in which we grow old depends upon each of us. Through our own actions and with the aid of our innermost resources, we can turn our advancing years into a fulfilling adventure, a time of growth, not of decline.

Between letting go of our youth and accepting our inevitable death, there is a time when we may feel deeply happy and free. That time is a unique opportunity to discover aspects of ourselves that we did not know, to see, to feel, and to love in a new way. Instead of becoming embittered, unattractive old people, we can hope to surround ourselves with joy and human warmth.

It is not a matter of idealizing old age, but of revealing what deserves to be revealed, without sentimentality and without complacency.

# WHEN THE FEAR OF
# GROWING OLD ASSAILS YOU

I recently celebrated my sixtieth birthday and am now a senior citizen. What's more, I have applied for a pass that will enable me to travel on public transport at a reduced fare. So I am officially entering my old age — my young old age, really, for I am in good health, active, and busy with a host of different projects. But, all the same, it is old age, and if all goes well, it will lead into extreme old age.

On the day I turned sixty, I recalled a scene from my childhood. I was fifteen at the time. A favorite aunt of mine came into the sitting room where my father was peacefully smoking his pipe, seated in an Empire-style wing chair upholstered in golden velvet. "Jean, I've just turned fifty!" she cried. "That's it! I'm old. Men won't turn and look at me as I walk past them in the street anymore!"

My aunt made a great impression upon

me, for she was tall and beautiful, and had great presence. She had completed her college entrance exams late in life, with the intention of studying psychology at university; she wanted to be a psychoanalyst. I admired her courage, her determination, and her clearheadedness. When I heard her that day, I told myself that when I was fifty, I, too, would be old. But when I reached that age, I remembered that scene and laughed, as I had never felt so alluring and self-confident. Old age seemed a very long way away.

Ten years later, I am beginning to understand what my aunt meant. It's not true that birthdays don't change anything; they are important symbolic stages. I am experiencing my admission into the ranks of sexagenarians as a kind of bereavement, with sudden attacks of sadness and a desire to do nothing, to fold in upon myself. It has to be said that I am going through some real bereavements, too: a painful divorce, and a love affair that ended in disappointment. I feel alone and vulnerable.

I have attempted to get closer to my children, but I'm well aware that it's not their job to carry my loneliness, for they have their own lives.

So I sit down at my desk and try to impose

some order upon my research, to analyze the articles I have collected over the past few months. The information I have obtained about old age doesn't help to reestablish my joie de vivre, for the books I read present me with a very bleak image of old age — giving me the impression that in our world, being "old" is a fault. In his speech at the UNESCO Congress in May 1998, Nobel laureate Elie Wiesel roundly denounced the ageism that is rampant in our youth-oriented society, and summed up all the unhappiness of being old: "The old? Their job is just to stay at home and not get in the way. They should be content that they're fed, clothed, and kept warm. . . . By turning them into recluses, we make them feel that they are excess baggage. As victims of a permanent system of humiliation, they cannot but feel ashamed that they are no longer young and in fact ashamed that they are still alive."

This contempt for the elderly is so strong that some very old people feel they are no longer worth anything. They would rather die than go on living with this loss of self-esteem, and I can understand why. When you are constantly being told that you are a burden on your family, or when you have become invisible to the world, why stay alive?

This fear of becoming a burden to loved ones is shared by the majority of people in my generation. We know that the older we become, the more we are perceived as burdensome. One day our children and grandchildren may perhaps feel that we are costing them too much. Will they then try to exert pressure on us to make way for them, as people did in former times in poor societies?

This brings to mind Imamura's film *The Ballad of Narayama.* In the Middle Ages in certain regions of Japan, it was the custom for elderly people to go and die alone in the forest, in order to spare the young the cost of having extra mouths to feed. In Canada in the days before the government instituted social-protection laws for the Inuit, the oldest would go off alone to die in the ice fields, although not before selecting a pregnant woman in the family circle in order to be reincarnated in the child she was carrying.

In his book *Still Here: Embracing Aging, Changing, and Dying,* Richard Alpert, alias Ram Dass, tells a story that clearly illustrates this fear that exists in us:

A Chinese story I love points this out

33

beautifully. It tells of an old man who's too weak to work in the garden or help with household chores. He just sits on the porch, gazing out across the fields, while his son tills the soil and pulls up weeds. One day, the son looks up at the old man and thinks, "What good is he now that he's so old? All he does is eat up the food! I have a wife and children to think about. It's time for him to be done with life!" So he makes a large wooden box, places it on a wheelbarrow, rolls it up to the porch, and says to the old man, "Father, get in." The father lies down in the box and the son puts the cover on, then wheels it toward the cliff. At the edge of the cliff, the son hears a knock from inside the box. "Yes, Father?" the son asks. The father replies, "Why don't you just throw me off the cliff and save the box? Your children are going to need it one day."[1]

Nowadays, our fear of being "eliminated" when we become too old and useless, too heavy a burden for society to bear, is a constant presence in our nightmares. And there is a direct link between contempt for the elderly and the feelings of loneliness and exclusion that so many older people experience. The burden of Alzheimer's disease, for example, falls to a large extent upon families, who sometimes have to sell their possessions in order to pay for institutional care for an elderly relative stricken with this illness.

So why did I hear the French philosopher André Comte-Sponville ask one day, Why shouldn't the lives of those who request death be shortened?[2] Why should we not legalize the option of granting death to those who no longer wish to be a burden to others? There is a clear economic argument in favor of euthanasia, but is this really the solution that our society wants to embrace?

In twenty years' time, much of the West will consist of continents of old people. This inversion of the age pyramid will endanger government budgets and pensions, employment prospects, and the comfort of younger generations. A ratio of one working adult per pensioner has been cited, which represents an extreme financial burden for our children and grandchildren. This cannot last. There will be a clash of interests and consequently a painful conflict. According to the French journalist François de Closets, we are heading for an intergenerational war:

The new generation will have to pay

for their children's education, their parents' retirement, their grandparents' extremely heavy health-care costs, the debts contracted by the preceding generations, and the retirement of foreign shareholders! They will work like madmen, under appalling pressure, in the hope of swiftly reaching the blessed moment when they can finally be paid for by their own children! What a wonderful outlook! Can we imagine everyone between the ages of fifty-eight and one hundred being a pensioner? It's obvious that such a system cannot work.[3]

It would be wise to heed François de Closets' words, for we must indeed plan for the financial shock of growing older.

When I first suggested to my publisher that I might write about aging well, I intended to write about the radiance of old age, about the dynamism of one's senior years. I had in mind a few wise sayings, such as Cocteau's: "I love growing old; age brings calm, equilibrium, altitude. Friendship and work take up all the room"; or the words spoken by Rita Levi-Montalcini, winner of the Nobel Prize for medicine: "Old age is, for me, the most beautiful period of my life."

I thought also of the words of a university

professor stricken with Charcot's syndrome, taken from *Tuesdays with Morrie:* "Growing old is not just deterioration, it is growth."[4] It was this serene, luminous face of old age that I wished to encounter.

But later on, I was overwhelmed with shame. I couldn't do it. I felt totally paralyzed in my writing, old and worn out before my time. I had always regarded life with an air of confidence, but now, as I entered the "third age," the specter of loneliness struck me down — plunged me, in a way that surprised even me, into unexpected depression.

In this detestable state of mind, I was rendered incapable of writing. Moreover, I barely recognized myself, overcome as I was with sadness and lethargy. I realized that the subject of my book kept bringing me back to the problem of isolation, of loneliness, so it was particularly difficult for me to tackle it in such a state. I needed to be capable of feeling a degree of optimism, even enthusiasm, a "warmth of the heart" — all of which evaporated that summer. At that moment, each thought I had about old age made me feel that I was plunging ever deeper into a colorless world. I could feel the anguish of my contemporaries. What's more, when I ventured to ask the elderly what they thought of old age, how they regarded it, I read fear in their eyes. Their faces became expressionless. Faced with their embarrassed silence, I swiftly understood that no one wanted to tackle a subject that was quite clearly sad and depressing.

# The Worst Is
## Not Inevitable

That summer passed, and I was unable to write a single line. And then two events set me back on track. The first was a horseback ride in the Camargue, a beautiful region between the Mediterranean Sea and the Rhône River delta in the south of France; the second, a meeting with the psychogeriatrician Olivier de Ladoucette.

I had promised my granddaughter Marie that I would take her to the Camargue for her tenth birthday. It is the region my grandmother came from, and we love it for its immense sky, the silvery light of its marshes, and its white horses.

We always stop off at the Hôtel de Cacharel, at Les-Saintes-Maries-de-la-Mer. It is run by Florian, the son of Denys Colomb de Daunant, whom we have to thank for that wonderfully poetic film that all French children know from fifty years ago: *White Mane*.

On this particular day, Florian took us horseback riding in the marshes that border his estate. It was warm, and the light was magnificent. In the distance, a few pink flamingos were fishing elegantly. It was a moment of peace. Our horses walked into the watery gray marshes. Splashes of water sparkled in the sunlight. Marie was happy. I could see her in front of me, beautiful and straight-backed, sitting well in the saddle. Suddenly my horse, Flamand, stopped in his tracks as his legs sank into the mud, right up to his belly. I called to Florian, who was astonished. He had no idea there was a hole at that spot in the marsh. After leading Marie to the bank, he came back for me, but I swiftly realized there was nothing he could do; he would sink into the mud as well. We went through all the possible solutions. The horse, he said, could get out on his own. But what about me? I couldn't dismount, and I couldn't swim, because there wasn't enough water. He could throw me a rope from the bank and I could maybe just about grab it and let myself be pulled out. I thought things over, still astride my trapped horse as he softly panted for breath. What if I left it up to the horse? Yes, said Florian, you can try, but you'll have to hang on tightly to the saddle, because when he decides to get out of the hole, things will get violent. I decided to give it a try. Two vigorous jabs of my heels, and my horse understood. He attempted a first leap forward, then a second, then a third. The leaps were jerky, but I hung on, and at last we were on the bank, our hearts racing, covered in mud, but happy to be out.

That evening, as I thought over this strange episode, I realized that life had just taught me a vital lesson.

The horse often appears in dreams as a symbol of strength and vitality. When it is white, it symbolizes spiritual energy. Jungian analysts see it as a figure of vital endeavor. I thought about how I was bogged down in the muddy waters of my own fear of growing older, incapable of moving forward, already old, and how that morning's event had shown me that by trusting my inner dynamism, my *conatus* — by trusting the life that still carries me — I could emerge from the bog of my depression.

On my return from the Camargue, I felt life returning, and I resumed writing this book. I had a twofold challenge to tackle, as I mentioned in my introduction: not to idealize old age but to help my generation get beyond its fears and advance toward old age as if it were an opening filled with light.

In view of the fact that we are promised increasingly long lives, let us search for the keys to inner youthfulness: a state of mind that will help us to avoid "rusting," that will prevent us from withdrawing into ourselves and enable us to retain vast horizons even if our physical world shrinks; in short, to remain alive right to the end.

Now that I was back in the saddle, so to speak, I decided that I wanted to meet Olivier de Ladoucette, because he has always regarded growing old in a way that is both knowledgeable and optimistic. He knows the subject well, as he teaches a psychology of aging course at Paris V University. He treats patients whom he describes as "young people from sixteen to ninety," and is a consultant at the Villa d'Épidaure, an establishment for patients suffering from Alzheimer's disease.

"People view the years that lie before them in a sad way," he told me. "I try to make them understand that growing old today can be experienced as a victory."

"A victory! Is that something our society can understand?" I asked. "Aren't we too resolutely pessimistic?"

"It is still difficult to adopt such a line of reasoning, but more and more people are listening. That doesn't mean that they're convinced, though. When you talk to them, they tell you that you're right, and then, five minutes later, they contradict you. I sense that they are still strongly influenced by the ideas that dominate in society: what is the point of growing old if we are all going to end up like vegetables!"

Olivier told me that not a single women's magazine wanted to write about his first book, *Bien vieillir* (Aging Well).

"I was given to understand that the word *aging* was an obscenity. The magazines were aimed at housewives under fifty! Three years later, when I brought out my second book, *Rester jeune, c'est dans la tête* (Staying Young Is All in the Mind), *Elle* magazine came and sought me out."

"Doubtless pressure from the baby boomers had something to do with it?" I asked him.

"Yes. Today we can talk about sixty-year-olds. We want to see them endowed with the qualities of seduction, youthfulness, vitality. It is still a little caricatured, focusing on a few stars, but at least we can identify with them. In ten years' time, we'll be able to talk about seventy-year-olds without any problems.

"What is still mysterious," Olivier went on, "is the fact that people don't perceive growing old as a progressive process but as something that 'attacks' you around the age of seventy-five or eighty. Between fifty and seventy-five, we don't know what is going on. We don't know what people are experiencing. We don't know who they are. They are probably afraid of growing old; they try to prolong their youth and they don't want to plan too much because they think things will go badly. They have realized that if they don't do too many stupid things, they can remain fit until they're seventy-five or eighty, but after that they are convinced that it will end badly and that their existential ticket beyond that limit will be seriously compromised."

"But isn't there a grain of truth in that?"

"Personally, I say no. A person can still be in good condition after the age of seventy-five. The increase in life expectancy is not an increase in the expectancy of a dependent life, but an increase in the expectancy of a healthy life."

"But there is a moment when things go downhill, and one goes into a serious decline, and sometimes this takes place over a long time."

"Yes, but that end period is going to arrive later and later, and it will also be increasingly short. We are living longer in good health, and then we are declining more quickly, and later. So we must reassure people who are afraid of an interminable end. This translates into very simple statistics: life expectancy is growing less quickly than the expectancy of a life without disabilities. So there is no need to panic. Of course, aging well demands that you have a healthy life, stay physically active, eat well, and have a social life. And you can't improvise all this at the age of seventy-five. You must be thinking about it from the age of sixty.

"When I tell people that they are going to live to a hundred, they are terrified. But I point out to them that they won't grow old the way their parents did. They have made different life choices, they have different ways of eating and doing sports, and they have access to medical care that didn't exist in earlier times. They have different ways of dealing with problems, of prioritizing leisure activities and enjoying themselves. Their parents lived through wars, they frequently didn't have enough to eat, they all smoked, and they didn't play sports.

"We are living in a society that hasn't realized that the physiological age and the social or subjective age no longer coincide. We talk about 'old people,' but that covers a wide variety of subgroups. This fifty-five-to-eighty age bracket is brand-new. It is up to our generation to explore a new way of growing old."

I was happy to hear Olivier de Ladoucette confirm my initial intuition. We then talked about the example of the centenarians on the island of Okinawa. Olivier was quite convinced that the heart does not age. Right to the end of a very long life, one can experience genuine surges of emotion and, in certain cases, even retain a sex life.

"It is much more active than one might imagine. It is a factor in equilibrium and longevity. Look at retirement homes! It's a totally taboo subject, but the reality is very touching. There are affectionate rapprochements, amorous impulses, even among dementia patients. The staff who work in retirement homes accept the residents' private lives relatively well. It is the families who are most intolerant. When their widowed papa starts flirting with Mrs. So-and-so, takes her by the hand and kisses her on the mouth, that embarrasses the children a great deal and they exert pressure for the culprits to be separated. This attitude on the part of the children clearly displays the difficulty we all have in visualizing our parents' sexuality.

"People imagine," Olivier continued, "that once we are past a certain age, we lose interest, that life no longer has any meaning and nothing makes us happy anymore. They are mistaken. They do not realize that as they grow older, their psyche evolves. Things that are unimportant when we are young take on an incredible importance when we grow older: a child's smile, for example. For an eighty-year-old, it's worth as much as a good three-star banquet when you're forty. You're no longer in the same space and time; you no longer have the same points of reference."

"Do you meet many people who are happy at an advanced age?"

"Yes, some even tell me that they are happier today than they were twenty years ago."

"But then why do so many elderly people commit suicide?"

"The fact that it's possible to be happy and old doesn't mean that all old people are happy — far from it. I believe that apart from the loneliness and possible mistreatment of our elders, they suffer above all because of the way we view them. They have the disastrous impression that they have become useless, transparent. It is absolutely vital that we stop seeing them as a burden to society."

47

I talked briefly about the fears we all have of becoming a burden to society. Olivier pointed out to me that the economic prospects are not as bleak as some might wish us to believe. First, the expenditure linked to growing old will be compensated for by a reduction in other social expenditures — such as on family allowances, education, and unemployment benefits — as the number of people of an age to procreate, train, and work will continue to diminish. Next, we must not forget the pool of jobs that will be created in the years to come through the management of old age and dependency. Last, senior citizens are excellent consumers and are reputed to be generous with their children and grandchildren.[1]

Returning to the feeling that the old are useless, Olivier stressed:

"We must learn to call on them, to appreciate everything that they can bring to us in terms of compassion, wisdom, time, and spirituality. It is clear that the countries that have the lowest numbers of suicides among the elderly — such as ultra-Catholic Ireland, England, and also the Nordic countries — have a real policy of taking responsibility for retired and elderly people. In these countries, the 'old' have their place, and a certain unity between the generations exists."

"Basically, in France, we grow old for a long time because our medicine is good and the environmental, economic, and cultural factors favor longevity," I suggested. "But we're not happy about getting old! One has the feeling that people get old in spite of themselves, and even we can do this better."

"Exactly!" Olivier agreed. "What can we do to ensure that our elders retain the feeling that they are worth something, that they are still useful? What can we do to make them feel less rejected, less unloved?"

As I took my leave of Olivier, I had the feeling that the future is bound to be less somber than we think. We will grow old for longer, but in a better way. We still have to construct a more positive image of this time of life, confront our fears in order to overcome them, and work out a real policy for preventing unhappy old age. Last, it is up to us to combat the denial of old age and death, by working at growing old.

# THE GOLDEN AGE
## OF SENIOR CITIZENS

A drawing by the cartoonist Georges Wolinski that appeared in the *Paris Match* shows a
group of healthy, laughing senior citizens,
happy to be alive and sharing a bottle of
wine in a bistro.[1] At the next table is a group
of young people, shoulders bowed, looking
sad and at a loss. A child is commenting on
the scene: "Seventy, that's the age when life
begins! The old folk make the most of the
time they have left. They go to the gym,
travel, and joke about their past." He points
out that the young people are having no fun:
"Look at them, they're grim-faced, un-
shaven, with their shirts hanging out of their
trousers. They don't know how to read,
write or express themselves anymore . . .
their girlfriends are Goths, tattooed and
pierced." Before concluding, he says: "You
can't imagine how much I'm looking forward to becoming a senior citizen!"
Wolinski has skillfully depicted this new

youth of robust and carefree "happy grand-dads and grandmas," who travel the globe on guided tours, enjoy a life of comfort and idleness, have the time to improve their minds by joining third-age clubs, and purchase staggering quantities of antiaging creams and pills to combat free radicals.

For our generation's obsession is, in fact, to stay young — a fact that the cosmetics companies and pharmaceutical and food-producing firms have clearly understood. They exploit the immense market represented by senior citizens and their fear of growing old. Seniors have money, so they and their wallets are a source of potential revenue; in short, they are ideal consumers. *Turning Silver into Gold: How to Profit in the New Boomer Marketplace* and *Ageless Marketing* — these are titles of recently published marketing guides aimed at so-called "seniors marketing." We don't want to get old, and we now have the means not to. We can slow down the aging process, as this L'Oréal advertisement for its Plenitude brand declares: "Intensely recharged during the night, the skin is fortified and regenerated on waking." We can act upon our bodies to give them every chance for a long life, and prevent them from clogging up and rusting too quickly.

Science now better understands how and why our cells break down and oxidize, how, in fact, they rust. It has been demonstrated that the restriction of calorie intake has an influence upon longevity, and our generation is reaping the benefits. We are eating less and better. There is talk of a "food consensus," the rules of which are: Drink water; banish tobacco, coffee, and most alcohol; reduce one's intake of animal fats, but consume good oils (olive, rapeseed, and fish); and eat lots of fruit — especially apples, which are like sponges to cholesterol — and vegetables.[2] We are adopting this consensus all the more easily because we can continue to drink red wine in moderation and eat chocolate. Red wine, which is very high in tannin, contains resveratrol, that mysterious molecule that protects against heart problems and prolongs life. We also know — and my friend Istvan d'Eliassy, owner of the Jadis and Gourmande chocolate house, confirms this — that dark chocolate is an antidepressant, for it contains magnesium and small quantities of serotonin. We know that it stimulates the production of endorphins, the brain's natural opiates, and that it also contains those famous antioxidants, which slow down the aging process. Already we have seen "antiaging chocolate" come onto the market, proving that marketing to seniors is in good health.

While our longevity depends upon our frugality and what we eat, it also depends to a large extent upon getting regular exercise. We know that walking often, cycling, jogging in good shoes, doing gymnastics and yoga, and climbing stairs instead of taking the escalator will help us to live better and longer.

We are being told about all kinds of scientific miracles that may prolong our lives, such as intelligence pills, and silicon chips implanted under the skin to replace defective organs. Longevity will, without a doubt, be one of the great themes of research to be carried out in the near future, and this will have a considerable economic impact.

The chapter that Joël de Rosnay devotes to this question in *Une vie en plus* (Another Life) is an exciting one.[3] In it we learn that in the United States, dozens of companies have already been set up to produce and sell products promoting longevity. Some businesses are searching for longevity genes by studying the genetic makeup of centenarians. In addition to longevity, prevention is another buzzword in scientific research. For instance, the Probiox laboratory in Belgium has perfected a method for visualizing the state of oxidization of the body's principal molecules. This is easily done through a simple blood test. One can find out if one's body is too oxidized, too rusted-up, and take the necessary measures: go on a diet, get involved in a sport, or avoid this or that other drug.

In this same spirit, we are probably heading toward the implantation of computer chips under the skin containing miniature medical files or reacting to metabolic disorders, and toward "intelligent textiles" capable of detecting heart rate, blood pressure, and the composition of sweat. Implants will be fitted, such as those mini-defibrillators that are already being worn by a few privileged individuals in the United States. These can detect a deficient heartbeat and respond with an immediate electrical discharge.

When our organs are worn out, we will replace them, just as we change the defective parts of a car. Either they will be reconstituted from embryonic human stem cells, or skin cells will be taken, "despecialized," and then transformed into specialized cells (muscle, bone, heart, etc.). This "tissue engineering technique represents an immense hope."[4] In the future, to make things simpler, organs will be reconstituted and then made to regrow inside the body.

One can also imagine entering into bodily "maintenance contracts" with certain pharmaceutical businesses linked to insurance companies. "A biological test could be carried out at home, using a strand of hair, a drop of blood, or a cell from the inside of the cheek, and then the results would be sent to a care center. By means of a telephone link, the home-assistance service would ensure that these were followed up," adds Joël de Rosnay, although he wonders about the indecent luxury of such a prevention service and the enormous divide that would then exist between the industrialized nations, where these kinds of maintenance contracts would become commonplace, and developing countries, where mortality would still remain high, owing to a lack of drinkable water and access to health care.[5]

All of this is both fascinating and frightening. One can imagine the monstrous narcissism of the old people we will be in the future, covered in prostheses and stuffed with computer chips that will notify our position to the doctor, diffuse such and such a hormone, and give us an electric shock if our heart falters. Not only will we have become veritable machines, but in addition, obsessed by our shape and our appearance, we will be solely and constantly preoccupied with ourselves and our sacred maintenance. One may suspect that such a development will only deepen the divide between rich pensioners and poor pensioners, as well as between older and younger generations.

This "new age" so envied by Georges Wolinski's young boy may be reduced to a time of carefree, selfish enjoyment. But as long as staying young depends on us — on our way of living and on our physical health — it is our responsibility to avoid two stumbling blocks.

The first consists of cutting ourselves off from the younger generations. This is what the humorist has grasped so well. There is something indecent about flaunting one's comfort, one's idleness, in front of young people who are having such a hard time finding work and getting a start in life. Our generation of baby boomers benefited from the post–World War II economic upturn, and it is undoubtedly the only generation that will benefit so extensively from the system put in place for retired people.

Recently, I overheard some young people chatting in a bar. They were talking about the precariousness of their jobs and their difficulties in finding somewhere to live, and then the conversation turned to the profound irritation they felt at the arrogance and selfishness displayed by a group of senior citizens who were talking loudly at the next table.

Georges Wolinski is quite right. The young are worried about their future and will no longer put up with the gilded image that we display. They will be even less willing to tolerate it given that everywhere it's being drummed into them that the fragile balance between the generations is about to collapse and that the "young will have to pay for the old."

The second stumbling block is that in obsessively trying to prolong our youth, we fail in our task of preparing ourselves for old age and death. The myth of eternal youth may prevent us from accepting the reality of growing old and knowing how to die when the moment comes.

How can we enjoy this golden age for senior citizens without coming up against one of these stumbling blocks? How can we take advantage of the formidable progress made in science and stay healthy for as long as possible without retreating into an unbearable, pathetic childishness? How can we make the best use of our longevity and accomplish this final task of growing old? For it is less about prolonging our lives indefinitely — something which in and of itself would be suffocating both for others and for ourselves — than about finding the keys to an inner youth and making the most of the time we have left to live.

# CHANGING THE WAY WE SEE

Olivier de Ladoucette, who sees hundreds of senior citizens every year, is quite categorical: people are afraid of growing old because they cannot bear the way other people will see them. Old people are made to feel that they are an ugly, useless burden on society. So we must begin by changing the way we see old people. Once we have done so, we will have a clearer understanding of how to ease our own fears.

In Africa and Asia, the old form a natural part of the landscape; in Western societies, though, we tend to hide them, simply because we consider them ugly. Armelle Canitrot rightly remarked in the newspaper *La Croix* that the black-and-white photos that used to depict our elderly "in a quasi-mystical light," with their expressive, wizened faces, have today been replaced by color photos of senior citizens in great shape. They show "Super-gran or -granddad with a good complexion, good skin, white teeth and graying temples, having a ball on vacation or riding a bike across a green meadow where the sun always shines. Those who have wrinkles or are aged over seventy-five need not apply."[1]

Samuel Bollendorff, director of the film *Ils venaient d'avoir 80 ans* (They Just Turned 80), confirms that no television channel wanted to show his film, which depicts very old people and gives them a chance to be heard. There is no question of "burdening the visual field" with images attesting to the inevitable losses and degradations of the "fourth age" — an age that is systematically associated with illness, ugliness, mental decline, isolation, boredom, and uselessness. Old people are alone, ill, and are going to die. And because the elderly are no longer productive, because their strength is declining and they no longer say much, because they have no political weight, do not defend their rights, and do not make themselves heard, we end up regarding them as worthless. The entire tragedy of old people's sadness derives from the shame they feel at being old and diminished, the feeling that they are no longer lovable, and the idea that they inspire disgust and fear in others.

That was the case with the eighty-year-old

woman who once sat next to me at the hairdresser's. As the stylist finished blow-drying her hair, I observed her out of the corner of my eye. She was a tall, distinguished woman, very thin and tastefully dressed, with a slender, lined face. Her features were regular; her profile, elegant. I told myself: How beautiful she must have been! And as the thought entered my mind, I wondered why she was no longer beautiful. I saw her sad expression in the mirror as she questioned it with large, anguish-filled eyes. She patted her hollow cheeks and gave a sigh that weighed a ton. "I don't have a face anymore," she whispered.

I imagined how this same face might look if it were lit up by a smile, the eyes sparkling with joy, like those of Irene Sinclair, the ninety-six-year-old model who posed for the cosmetic brand Dove and whose face is deeply lined yet radiant.

Then I realized what some old people lack — the missing factor that would make them beautiful. It isn't smooth skin or rounded cheeks; it is joy and youthfulness of heart.

But we all know that as long as magazines and books place all their emphasis upon the vital importance of remaining young, we will continue to have a choice between just two equally somber prospects.[2] Either we can remodel ourselves, constantly toning our muscles, resorting to advances in cosmetics and aesthetic surgery, in order to slow down the process of growing old and conserve a semblance of youth, or we can resign ourselves to the inevitable and hide.

We need to stop gazing fearfully at the aesthetic criteria of youth and implement a narcissistic revolution. We need to discover the extraordinary freedom we will gain once we stop being preoccupied with our own image, with other people's vision of us. Until then, we will continue to die in fear.

It seems to me that it would be much more intelligent and fulfilling to learn how to see with the eyes of the heart. Then perhaps the face of old age will appear natural and — why not? — even enviable.

## Rethinking Our Aesthetics

During a seminar devoted to the question of "the body in old age," Danielle Bloch, the art historian, showed a series of slides depicting the bodies of old men and women in Western art.[3] These were difficult images to look at, portraying the naked body at an advanced stage of life, with all its creases, sagging flesh, baggy skin, missing teeth, and eyes that were red-rimmed or as moist as lakes. The realism was terrifying. It is true that from the point of view of the objective body, of corporeality, old age is indeed ugly.

The experts invited to this seminar felt pain, as did I. All of us, with the exception of one or two, were aged over sixty, and it felt as though we were being shown our own reflections in a mirror — being presented with an image of what we perhaps already were, or what we were about to become. Were they really mine, those facial wrinkles, that sagging skin under the arms, that bald head, that flabby belly, those legs covered in varicose veins? How could we overcome this sadness at the prospect of a withering body and accept this damage to our self-image?

Without question, we must bid farewell to our bodies' objective beauty. Despite advances in aesthetic surgery, cosmetics, and public health, they will wear out, even if we play sports and watch what we eat. There's no doubt about it. We cannot escape this period of bereavement.

Once we accept that we are going to lose something, something new comes along. That is the way bereavement works. This is reality, not consolation, but we forget that. So I sincerely believe that we can succeed in loving ourselves beneath our wrinkles, beneath the folds and pockets of our skin. Our narcissistic wounds will heal, and then others will see another kind of beauty within us.

During the discussion that followed the slide show, the philosopher Bertrand Vergely exclaimed: "But aren't there any depictions of the beauty of old people?" Alas, no. The West seems to have opted for a strictly terrifying depiction of the body, as if to remind man that where the body is concerned, all is vanity. Bertrand Vergely then pointed out that in the Orient, bodies are not displayed. Instead, faces are shown: faces that, although deeply lined by time, express fulfillment. He cited the magnificent faces of the old sadhus in India, the peaceful faces of old people in China, and the radiance of icons, which express a profound body, not simply one that is visible and corruptible. They teach us that it is possible to be aware of a body of light, the ontological double of the physical body. As for the old people of India or China who practice meditation and silence, they are also aware of this body, and that is why their faces fascinate us so much.

As I listened to him, the Dove advertisement for a range of antiaging products came back to me. In the advertisement, Irene Sinclair posed with a dazzling smile on her deeply lined face, and alongside her picture was a question: "Wrinkled or wonderful?" This question sums up the distinction we must make between the body (wrinkled) and what one might call "bodyness" (the way one exists within one's body — in this case, vividly).

This advertisement, in fact, went far beyond simply urging us to purchase the brand's products. It showed us the way. True, we must kiss our young skin good-bye and accept our wrinkles, but another kind of beauty is accessible to us — that of emotional youth. We can be radiant with joy, and our bodyness will gain the upper hand over our body. So it is possible to accept the image of oneself as an old man or old woman. Almost everything happens as if the physical transformation gradually forces the psychological apparatus to assimilate this change. This is what the psychoanalyst Gérard Le Goués jokingly calls the *stade des rides* (wrinkle stage).

In October 2005, couturier John Galliano appealed for elderly models for his 2006 spring and summer show. Modeling agencies, such as the famous Elite agency, requested the portfolios of models aged between sixty-five and one hundred. The models in the photos have eyes that sparkle with life, gray hair that shines brilliantly, and a jaunty tilt of the head. All of their faces are marked by time, but they have such character that an elderly customer will want to identify with the models, and young people can tell themselves that they would be very happy to grow old the way these women have.

Among the slides presented by Danielle Bloch, one image particularly intrigued me. It was of a painting by Andrès Serrano, dating from 1994, that depicts two elderly lovers, naked, facing each other. The sagging flesh and other signs of aging make this a difficult painting to look at, and yet the two lovers are still so alive, so full of joy at being together, that they seem totally unaware of the ugliness of their bodies. Is there a moment when growing older forces us to stop looking at our bodies vainly and, if we have not already done so, to learn to be aware of our bodies, to feel the pleasure of being alive through contact with another person, through the softness of their skin on our own?

At this seminar, as I reviewed the images we had been shown, I told myself that it was undoubtedly more respectful of oneself and of others to hide an old body. I thought of the old woman who comes every day of the year to a beach on the île d'Yeu to swim naked. She arrives early in the morning, when the beach is almost deserted, and undresses discreetly behind the rocks. I realize that she does not want to deprive herself of the pleasure of feeling the seawater on her skin, but she has accepted that her body is no longer "fit to be seen." She is careful in her undressing, not only through modesty but to spare others. And at the same time, she wishes to continue experiencing her body, to feel physical pleasure.

## The Beauty That Shines Through

On the one hand, people complain that old age is hidden away; on the other, they are satisfied with this arrangement because they consider age to be ugly. As I mentioned earlier, this paradox leads us to distinguish the "body one has" from the "body one is." It is the "body one has" that we may hide, out of respect for ourselves and for others, but the "body one is" then runs the risk of disappearing as the elderly body is kept out of sight. How can we show the physicality of elderly men and women, depict their way of existing in their bodies? Having an old body does not prevent one from being happy in one's body, or from experiencing pleasure through that body.

It is fortunate that nowadays international

associations such as Little Brothers of the Poor have realized that action needs to be taken to change the image of old age, to alter mind-sets. Little Brothers of the Poor appealed to photographer Hien Lam Duc to challenge the idea that it is shameful to show old age. It is not a question of idealizing it but of showing what it is: a face is always the reflection of a state of mind. To show old age is to show people who are full of experiences and emotions, who have a whole depth of life in their faces. We can read the emotional lives of the elderly in their faces: their loneliness, their tiredness, but also their serenity, their impulses, and their desires. For their desires are still there — they have simply been transformed. Tenderness has replaced seduction.

The interest of Hien Lam Duc's photographs derives from the fact that he shows clearly how the quality of one's relationship with an old person can be seen on that person's face, enabling attention, respect, and tenderness to shine through.

### Yvonne
*Il n'y a que toi et les oiseaux* (Just You and the Birds) is a magnificent book, illustrated with fifty black-and-white photos, that celebrates the beauty of old age. Its author,

Michel Bony, was twenty-two at the time of writing and lived in an eight-square-meter attic room in the Temple district of Paris, traveling back and forth from his room to his theater classes at the circus, where he performed in a show. His neighbor was Yvonne, a woman, then aged ninety-two, with whom he built up a rare friendship.

"As for ninety-two-year-old Yvonne, she spent most of her time in her room, reading, writing, listening to the radio, preparing her meals, but above all dreaming and reciting — both for the beauty of the words and in order to continue exercising her memory — a speech by Corneille, a poem by Rimbaud, or even a prayer to the good Lord. For although she was a believer, she had long since come to believe that the house of God dwells in the hearts of men."[4]

Michel Bony's photos reveal the wrinkles, the white hair, the wear and tear, but also the grandeur and humor of a very dignified old lady.

He amassed the photos during their ten years of friendship. One day, as he was showing them to his friends, he realized that they were "the most stinging riposte to de Gaulle ('Old age is a shipwreck'), to Mauriac ('There is no such thing as a beautiful old person'), and to all those who feel pity or fear, or turn their heads away when they see those who are too old."[5]

The text that accompanies the photographs expresses the singularity of this friendship, which profoundly changed the author. "I would not be who I am today without her affectionate listening and the way she had of taking the heat out of the smallest situations." He goes on to say: "Yvonne had an incredible appetite for life. She taught me Hope. Thanks to her, I now have a different relationship with old age, starting with my own.

"Talking was no longer enough for us. We went as far as passing a notebook from door to door, in which jottings on death, love, and humility were interspersed with newspaper articles and recipes."[6] Yvonne passed away at the age of one hundred.

One day we shall be able to look at pictures of old people and be moved. We will unreservedly identify with them, and tell ourselves that we would love to be like them when we are old. On that day, our society will have taken a giant step forward.

"Should we be afraid of old age?" This is the question that the popular television program *L'Arène de France*[7] put one evening to a panel that was deemed to be representative of the French population, to which 73 percent answered yes. The program took place in the presence of a *grand témoin* (grand witness), Éric-Emmanuel Schmitt. On the panel were a government minister; a woman representing the private retirement homes' union; a philosopher; a woman who had had her face completely surgically lifted; another who for many years cared for her elderly mother, a victim of Alzheimer's disease, at home before reluctantly entrusting her to a retirement home; a technocrat from the École Polytechnique who was obsessed with eradicating old age and convinced that science would succeed in doing so; and, last, Tsilla Chelton, an eighty-eight-year-old actress who was so beautiful that she was the only person on the platform whom you noticed.

This was a program in which everyone talked about this and that without really listening. People interrupted one another, creating a real uproar that the chairman, Stéphane Bern, had a great deal of difficulty controlling. But that evening something happened, and I believe it helped France to make a significant advance. First, the program was brave enough to put old age front and center, and to allow old people to speak. Admittedly, they were "healthy, wealthy, and famous," as one participant remarked, and this is a remark that should be taken seriously. The program did not show the negative side of old age but merely alluded to it discreetly via the distressing testimony of the woman who eventually placed her mother in a retirement home — a testimony that showed us how very, very sad that world is. The faces on the platform changed. There was a feeling that, for a second, everyone imagined themselves in that old woman's place and felt the horror of that sadness. Even the woman who was a director of a retirement home could not hide her emotion.

But the program's key moment — one might say its turning point — occurred when Tsilla Chelton began speaking. Her face bore the marks of time, as did her body, and she had made no attempt to hide them. There was something luminous about her, and this radiant presence asserted itself as she addressed the audience, seated on benches around the sides of the studio. "Growing old is interesting! Really interesting!" she said forcefully. "At last you are free! You are liberated from all those passionate affairs that demand so much energy!" The philosopher Roger Dadoun, aged ninety, who was present, had just written a manifesto for "an ardent old age." He didn't contradict her; in fact he, too, praised old age. Both of them wondered why whenever someone complimented them, they would say, "How young you are!" It would be more accurate to say, "What a beautiful old person you are!" One sensed that the panel was in agreement here: a man or a woman could be beautiful at any age. Another moving moment came when a young student in his twenties talked about living with a ninety-year-old woman whom he found "fascinating." Had all these testimonies succeeded in convincing the public that there was no need to be afraid of growing old? Yes, they had. When at the end of the program Stéphane Bern once again asked whether we should be afraid of growing old, 63 percent of the people answered no.

This courageous program also strengthened my belief that the media must show more positive experiences of old age. That evening proved that we can change the way we view old people and this time of life that we fear so much.

# Answering Fears About Old Age

After the *Arène de France* program, deeply impressed by the shift in opinion that I had seen take place in a public forum, I decided to go back and look individually at the fears and agonizing questions that had assailed me at the beginning of my investigation.

Many of us young senior citizens still have living parents who have reached greater old age. They do not always present us with an enviable picture of those later years. Some have become dependent or suffer from dementia, and we have taken the painful, guilt-ridden decision to place them in retirement homes or in specialized establishments. We do not have the necessary means to enable them to grow old at home with someone to take care of them, nor the determination to take them into our own homes. As we support our parents, there are lingering questions deep in our heart of hearts: Will we grow old alone, feeling useless? Will we, too, be parked in one of those ghettoes for the old that we call retirement homes? Will we end our lives in the dark night of dementia?

## Connecting Generations

I do not think we truly realize how much we have lost as a result of the sociological changes of the last few decades. Contact between grandparents and grandchildren occurred naturally in the era of extended families living under the same roof. Today, different age groups have become compartmentalized. How badly things have deteriorated to create a situation where we have to appeal to an association in order to establish affectionate links between the generations![1]

Even though there is still much to do if these residences for the elderly or those suffering from dementia are to be turned into real homes, many humane models already exist. It is heartening to know that the authorities are aware of the public-health issue that the aging population represents. They have already announced numerous plans, but it is up to us to ensure that they are followed up with concrete measures addressing the fears that dwell within us.

But none of these initiatives or plans will be effective unless our generation, that of the fifty-five-to-seventy-five age group, the pivotal generation between the oldest and the youngest groups of seniors, becomes aware of the importance of solidarity. We are the "strong link in the chain of solidarity," a French minister recently declared.[2] It is up to us to develop the good ideas that are flourishing all over the world, such as "cafés of the ages," which enable different generations to come together, or social housing that would bring together young couples with small children and retired people.[3] It is well known how much elderly people enjoy contact with the very young. I was convinced of this the day I saw a young woman place her six-month-old baby on her grandfather's bed as he lay dying in the hospital. I saw this old man, with his sad, lost expression, sit up, his face illuminated by a beautiful smile as joy filled his heart.

An American girlfriend told me that in one shopping mall in the United States, there is a public space where parents can leave their babies while they do their shopping. The young children are cared for by vetted elderly volunteers who are assisted by a qualified pediatric nurse.[4] It is easy to imagine the reciprocal benefits of such contact.

Jérôme, a young political science student whom I met recently while visiting friends, told me that he was lodging with an eighty-five-year-old woman in a large apartment in the Latin Quarter in Paris, under the French government's "One Roof, Two Generations" scheme. This plan is supported by the students at his school, who drew up the charter for the tenancy agreement, which is based upon a mutual understanding to abide by the policies of discretion, respect, trust, and tolerance. In return for his presence, and for small services such as changing lightbulbs and carrying up bottles of water, he is comfortably lodged in a bedroom with a connected bathroom. Three times a week, he spends the evening with this old woman, the widow of a law professor, who is very cultured but very lonely, for she has no children. Sometimes she takes him to a restaurant, but mostly they have dinner at home and listen to music or watch a film together. Sharing these moments of relaxation with a young man stimulates her. She feels younger. As for him, he is learning a great deal from her, for she has traveled extensively, and tells him humorous anecdotes about her adventures.

We are afraid of becoming invisible, of no longer being of interest to anyone. "The precious, important things you wanted to pass on no longer interest your descendants. As for your experience, it's quite simple, it bores the pants off them!" writes the French feminist author Benoîte Groult. "They don't expect surprises from us anymore, apart from heart attacks, broken hips, strokes or the slow horror of Alzheimer's. . . . How can we surprise them?" she wonders.[5]

It is indeed up to our generation to combat this sidelining of older people and to demonstrate the value that they can bring us. We could take our inspiration from an American experiment. In certain areas of New York, "elders' circles" have been set up to enable those who suffer from loneliness and feelings of uselessness to pass on their knowledge about life to younger generations. In these circles, the oldest people sit in the center and the youngest sit on the periphery. In accordance with the Native American tradition, a talking stick is placed in the center of the circle. Whenever they wish, the elders can fetch it and return to their seats. They share their experiences and their thoughts with the rest of the group. This leads to the creation of a collective wisdom, to which each person brings his or her contribution.

Claudine Attias-Donfut, the research

director of the National French Retirement Fund, is following up on a remarkable piece of work carried out in collaboration with the National Gerontology Foundation. It was suggested to people in their eighties and nineties that they write letters addressed to their grandchildren. These letters, produced by individuals who had been reduced to silence by our society, constituted an unprecedented document. Almost all the letters were written by women. In them, they spoke of their joys and woes, of their past and present lives. One of the letters in particular touched me, because it spoke to all of our consciences. It was from a woman aged ninety. She wrote to her "dear children," who, on her behalf, had made the decision to put her in a retirement home. "I would like to say to families: discuss things with your parents. It is their lives that you are manipulating. We are not toys. At our age, we take everything to heart; the merest thing can hurt us. So, if you please, do not regard us as puppets devoid of feelings as soon as we become burdensome. Talk to us. Let us take some part in our own lives. Thank you."[6]

We ask ourselves the most agonizing questions: What are we to do with our parents when they are no longer self-sufficient, when they can no longer drive their cars or do their shopping? And what about our children? What will they do with us when we reach that stage? That question worries us, for we would all like to grow old and die in our own homes, in the place where we feel most at ease. That is where our daily habits and our memories are based, where we can live life at our own pace and receive visits from whomever we choose. Many of us prefer the idea of growing old at home, even at the risk of falling ill or having an accident. However, even with the increased home help that exists today, even with the progress in robotics and arrangements for detecting falls, gas leaks, and other anomalies, the loss of physical and sometimes mental autonomy can make life at home impossible.

## Natural Caretaking

All the reports of unhappiness experienced by those who end their lives in institutions, and the poor reputations of retirement homes, have contributed to redressing the balance. Today, some families have no hesitation in taking an aged parent back home with them. In recent years in the United States, it has been estimated that only 4.1 percent of the population of those older than sixty-five live in institutions such as nursing homes, while an increasing number move in with immediate family. But this unity between children and parents represents an effort. It is a choice that implies strong constraints and a great deal of affection. That is why we must prepare ourselves for it; otherwise, reality will quickly overtake good intentions. Having an elderly parent at home can be so all-consuming that it can become unbearable, and this can lead to a kind of abuse within families. Living with an elderly parent is certainly possible, but on two conditions: that you are well organized, and that you get along well with the parent in question.

The public authorities are increasingly aware of the need to support what are known in France as *aidants naturels* (natural caretakers). Interesting developments in this direction include the financing of respite care, the creation of structures for temporary accommodations, and the evolution of voluntary help.

Some Belgian friends of mine who are very much involved in providing voluntary support have embarked upon an interesting experiment inspired by a program in Quebec: residential help.[7] The two of them stay at the homes of families who have a parent suffering from Alzheimer's and who need a vacation. They move in for a week or two and take complete care of the sick person. A log enables them to share daily events with the family on their return.

A couple of factors play an important role in the success of cohabitation: the personality of the elderly person brought into the home, and his or her ability to grow old well (that is, to accept the losses that age inflicts and grow emotionally from them, and to gain in stature each time conflicts, jealousies, or simple exhaustion pollute the situation).

Two years ago, a couple I know, Pierre and Georgina, decided to take in Chantal, Georgina's mother. Several falls, memory loss, and difficulties in doing her shopping marked the beginning of dependency. The couple thought long and hard about it. The relationship between mother and daughter was strong; the fact that Georgina had given up work, and the size of the house, enabled them to embark upon this adventure, or at least to attempt it. "I couldn't have lived with myself if I didn't try," Georgina confided to me.

So Chantal moved in. It wasn't easy for her, leaving her own place and moving in with her daughter. She was no longer at home. She experienced contradictory feelings: the well-being of feeling safe, of being in an intimate, loving atmosphere with her daughter and a son-in-law she liked, but also anxiety about the future. How would the situation develop as time went on, and as she lost more and more of her independence? She had a feeling of foreboding that little by little, the actions of daily life, such as managing her own affairs and her bank account, were going to escape from her grasp. How was her daughter going to feel about this reversal of roles when Chantal became, to some degree, her daughter's daughter? How was Pierre going to tolerate this permanent intrusion by a third party into their life as a couple? How would they manage to accept, without bitterness, the fact that they could no longer have vacations and weekends away, and that they would have to get up in the night to take care of her?

Although aware of the difficulties that might arise, Georgina and Pierre nevertheless chose to live in the present. What wisdom! For the moment, this upheaval in their life is amply compensated for by the richness of their relationship with Chantal. She is a gentle, patient woman who is able to accept help graciously, and it is a pleasure to look after her. She is undemanding, and makes good use of her smiles and her kisses, aware of the burden she represents.

One day, the couple may well have to place Chantal in an institution, and they have discussed this with her. But for the time being, they are concentrating on the good times.

From this example, we see how richly rewarding the experience of living together can be, albeit at a price. It demands a great deal of hard work and love.

## Sheltered Housing

Between the option of an old age spent at home, fraught with difficulties, and the retirement home, which inspires so much fear because to many people it is tantamount to imprisonment, an intermediate solution has evolved: that of sheltered housing. This enables residents to enjoy the self-respect of having their own space: a private room in which they can have their own furniture and the ability to live life at their own pace, coming and going as they wish. On the other hand, they also have the benefit of a shared space, should they wish to take their meals with other residents or participate in group activities.

A sheltered-housing project for retired

women has just been set up in Montreuil, and the story of the experiment is worth telling. Three seventy-year-olds have worked there for ten years.

La Maison des Babayagas (Babayagas' House) — a reference to Russian grandmothers — houses seventeen women aged over sixty, all of them widowed, single, or divorced. Each woman has a thirty-five-square-meter studio apartment, such as one would have in social housing. The ground floor comprises the shared areas dedicated to cultural or social events and group activities. A swimming pool is planned for the basement. This is a self-run, self-sufficient residence. In other words, it functions with a minimum of outside help, even in terms of medicine and housework, and it offers — but does not impose — a shared life and activities involving the outside world. It also divides up certain expenses in order to compensate for the reduced pensions of women who had to put children before work. It is "an anti–retirement home . . . a real bulwark against withdrawing into one-self."[8]

This is a fine project for women who want to remain free, who do not want to be a burden to their relatives, and who, above all, do not want to be treated like children.

These are women who want to fight against isolation and create a friendly, involved environment. Men can visit them but not live there.

The *babayagas* are suspicious of the power of doctors and the pathologization of old age. They think that "old people's illnesses are often illnesses of boredom and isolation."[9]

Their project is limited by the fact that it has not been designed to house women who are dependent or who suffer from an advanced degenerative illness. If one of the *babayagas* deteriorates to that point, she must be transferred to a home with medical supervision. But, as much as possible, the plan is for the able-bodied women to assist with the others' handicaps — a plan that is intended to unite these retired women in solidarity.

In order to deal with the inevitable conflicts that all communities experience, the founders — Thérèse, Suzanne, and Monique — came up with the idea of having regular visits from a woman mediator. "This project makes great demands on everyone. It must be clearly stated which matters are collective and which are private."[10]

The ambition of this "realist utopia" is to become part of an old-age movement that shakes up old Europe. Its founders would like it to be the inspiration for other projects elsewhere.

## The Beguine Convent

A good portion of this book was written in the little house I built on the île d'Yeu — a small island off the Vendée coast of France. The île d'Yeu was known for a long time as the first tuna-fishing port on the Atlantic coast, and is now a popular vacation destination in France. One night, at dinner with my friends on the island, we talked about our old age and where we would like to grow old. None of the dinner guests wanted to end their lives in an old people's home. Once again, I witnessed the horror that this thought inspires among men and women of my generation.

"We should come up with something like a Beguine convent," I suggested. "In medieval Belgium, widows got together in groups of eight to form a little community of aging individuals who had decided to help one another in this last phase of life. They lived alone, in little houses tightly packed together, around a church and a garden. The idea was to live together while respecting each individual's freedom, undertaking to share and to maintain solidarity. At that time, sharing revolved around gardening and religious worship. When one of them died, the others sat with her. Then they co-opted another Beguine.

"Since we love this island so much, and some of us are fortunate enough to have our own places here, and our houses are so close to one another's, why shouldn't we form a modern version of the Beguine convent — a mixed one, obviously? We could all live in our own homes, and have our own freedom, but we would dream up communal activities, walk around the island and do our gardening together; and why not meet up regularly to practice some kind of spiritual activity, such as meditation, or contemplation? And if one of us fell ill or even became dependent, we could take turns to help so that he or she could stay at home rather than go into an old people's home. There would be a contract of solidarity among us."

An extremely animated discussion ensued. Some people had no thoughts of growing old on the island. They wanted to travel *ad vitam aeternam* (for all time), crisscrossing the world's highways and byways, and more than anything did not want to become sedentary. One voice was raised to quote Baudelaire's poem "Le Voyage," which takes us from the limitless horizon of a child to the shrunken space of an old man: *"Une oasis d'horreur dans un désert d'ennui"* (An oasis of horror in a desert of boredom). The man who quoted this to us wondered if the island might not become that oasis of horror the moment he made the decision to stay there forever.

"But what will you do when you can't travel anymore?" someone asked. "You'll have to settle somewhere. So, where?" By the end of dinner, most of my friends who had met up that evening had rallied to the idea of a new kind of Beguine convent. It is true that the idea of planning to stay in one's own home, gradually over the years constructing a network strong enough to support one another in the event of dependency and even dementia, is a plan with merit. There are no financial or legal implications; everything rests on a moral contract.

Our host then wondered if the friendship that binds us today would be sufficiently strong and durable to stand the test of time and of our growing old. Someone mentioned the changes of character and mood in old people, who sometimes become unbearable. How could we be sure that we would retain our personalities? The spiritual bond between us would indeed have to be very strong. The medieval Beguines were united by religious practice, but that is not true in our case. Some of us believe in God; others don't. Some of us pray; others don't. So what do we have in common in terms of spirituality? We share the humanist values of respect and caring for others, a desire for solidarity, an appreciation of nature, an ability to marvel at the infinite diversity of the skies, a taste for silence, and, above all, the certainty that deep down, the most important thing is to love. Isn't that a sufficient spiritual connection?

The question has remained open. It is gaining ground. At any rate, in our eyes it seems preferable to those ghettoes for old people that current retirement homes can represent. However, one day we might have to steel ourselves to place a loved one in an institution. Perhaps our own children will have no other choice when it comes to us.

## Outsourcing Elder Care

One of my friends, who is the medical director of several establishments for patients suffering from Alzheimer's disease, went to Morocco recently to research the possibility of setting up retirement homes there. Why? Because large numbers of people could live out their retirement comfortably in a country where the cost of living is cheaper, and where there are no difficulties in finding staff who are competent, available, humane, and warm. But I have been told this poses an ethical problem: is it a good thing to export our elderly — to send them to live far from their own country and their children?

However, this is exactly what is being done in Japan, where there is a plan to export old people to "reserves" purchased on the east coast of Africa. This also takes place in the United States, where hundreds of deluxe community hospitals are being constructed. Sun City in Arizona is a closed housing development with secure districts. Its advantage is that senior citizens there feel protected against outside dangers, and the town also offers all sorts of services for people who are becoming dependent. Its disadvantage is that they are cut off from the world.

This doctor wondered if, despite the sun, the pleasant climate, and the kindness of the Moroccans, the old people who went to live in these retirement homes would suffer more from a feeling of being uprooted than those who stayed in France. By moving abroad, wouldn't they become cut off once and for all from their children? As I listened to him, I couldn't help remembering King Hassan II's observation that the advent of retirement homes in Morocco would signal the country's demise, because a country that abandons its family condemns itself to death.

That sentiment expresses the extent of the gulf that separates our rich countries, where the old no longer have a place, from the countries of the Maghreb, Africa, and Asia, where it would be unthinkable to sideline the elderly in such a way.

## Guiding Lights

I have been thinking about this eventuality on my own behalf. When it happens, I would like my children to help me choose a good establishment, one that is comfortable and cheerful, with a humane staff, and I would like us to take the time to visit several.

I would also like to have the time to prepare myself for this final move. The worst thing, it seems to me, would be to enter a retirement home one has not chosen, and against one's wishes. An inner acceptance must take place, and that requires time: time to accept that one is no longer self-sufficient, without feeling diminished by that fact; and time to accept that one must gratefully entrust one's body to other people's care. I have frequently observed how those who have the ability to do so with grace, without embarrassment or humiliation, can help their carers to look after them attentively and with respect. Grace, gratitude, and humor are the best guarantees of successful adaptation.

When the day comes, I would like to remember these words of Ram Dass, which have often made me laugh: "I have learned to love my wheelchair (which I nickname my gondola) and to enjoy being pushed along by attentive individuals. Chinese emperors and Indian maharajas were after all transported on palanquins! In other cultures, being carried and pushed is a sign of honor and power!"[11]

As I approach this time in my life, I would like to reread two works that will, I think, help me to remember that man's willpower is so great it can transform anything. As the philosopher Robert Misrahi put it so well, the old man who can no longer move around, who is housebound in a cramped space, bedridden, or confined to a chair, can turn that materially impoverished space into one that is "poetically transfigured."[12]

The first book is *Tuesdays with Morrie*, which I translated from the American English and prefaced in 1998.[13] It is the diary of an old university professor stricken with Charcot's syndrome, which progressively paralyzed him. In the face of this inescapable, painful shrinking of his space, the old man learned how to expand it, to perceive in fine detail everything that was physically beyond him, in a process that the philosopher Maurice Merleau-Ponty called the "miraculous continuation of the body." In this way, while remaining motionless in his bed, he experimented with his ability to sense things beyond himself, an ability that the Greeks called *hapsis*. He "smells" the tree that he can see through his bedroom window. He enjoys it. He "exists" in its branches and "feels" the wind caressing them. Thus, while becoming progressively more paralyzed, he experiments with a form of joyful freedom.

In the face of his almost total dependence, which is the worst of ills in a world that values mastery and control, the old man learned, he wrote, to "love it." He did so by rediscovering that former time when he enjoyed having people take complete care of him — a time that he never completely forgot. The old man confessed:

I began to *enjoy* my dependency. Now I enjoy when they turn me over on my side and rub cream on my behind so I don't get sores. Or when they wipe my brow, or they massage my legs. I revel in it. I close my eyes and soak it up. And it seems very familiar to me.

It's like going back to being a child again. Someone to bathe you. Someone to lift you. Someone to wipe you. We all know how to be a child. It's inside all of us. For me, it's just remembering how to enjoy it.

The truth is, when our mothers held us, rocked us, stroked our heads — none of us ever got enough of that. We all yearn in some way to return to those days when we were completely taken care of — unconditional love, unconditional attention. Most of us didn't get enough.[14]

Here the old professor offers us a completely original point of view on dependency and this freedom that we have to turn a shrunken, impoverished space into one that is "poetically transfigured."

The second book I would take away with me is *Le Cahier de Marie,* the diary of an old woman with a soft heart and a keen eye, written when she had just entered a retirement home.[15] She gives us portraits of her new friends, her neighbors, and the staff. By writing each Sunday night after dinner, she transforms the silence of curfew into "benevolent calm."

Far from withdrawing into herself, Marie observes, listens, and tries to understand the other residents. A whole life is laid out, both interior and exterior. She writes of trying to share the world of the most disoriented residents, such as Hubert, a poor old fellow who rocks back and forth, repeating, "We must hide, we must hide."

"After the afternoon nap, I shall go and sit next to Hubert. Last week, I sat down opposite him and I rocked, like him. He stopped; so did I. We looked at each other. And if I weren't afraid of big words, I would say that there was a meeting of souls."[16]

Marie had a marvelous way of looking at the things and people around her in this home — a way of looking that is full of life, humor, and affection. Always concerned about others, she took part in everything, from the pottery workshop to the celebrations, with good humor. She quickly stopped complaining about the imposed timetable of getting up, washing, meals, and activities, for in them she rediscovered the era of childhood. "The important thing is no longer to run to do something but to stop and dream, look at the sky, chat with the person next to you. It is to breathe in the smell of the coffee which insinuates itself into that of the disinfectant, to feel one's body, and converse with one's eyes."[17] However, she was not gentle about hypocrisy, about what was left unsaid, the hiding of death when it took away some resident or other, or the absence of farewell rituals.

The most touching thing about Marie's chronicle is the "spring-cleaning" she carried out inside herself, gently, according to the pace of the memories that came to her, the sorrows that had to be liberated, the forgiveness she needed to grant herself. "It is hard to forgive oneself. . . . When I think of all those people to whom I have caused sorrow, whom I have hurt, sometimes even without realizing it, now that I am old, I realize how important it is to be delicate. I would like to know if other people besides me feel the same thing."[18] In her old age, Marie wanted to find people to help her to think, to help guide her.

At times, waves of gratitude rose up inside her; the desire to say thank you to all those she had loved, to those she had encountered, for those thousand and one small things that had made a mark upon her life.

Everything depends upon the way we look

at life. Life in a retirement home could be horrible — the life of a concentration camp inmate. If you admit defeat, if you close yourself up, you may feel that you are in a place where everything is dead. But if you have an open heart, like Marie, it can be an opportunity for exchange, for affection, and for life.

Take this moving passage:

> Nathalie walked in. She came toward me and whispered: "Hello, Madame T., and happy birthday: it's your birthday today. The weather is wonderful." She half-opened the shutters. "It really is a beautiful summer's day." Nathalie sat down beside me. She asked me: "What would you like?" I answered: "I'd like you to wish me happy birthday." Then she did something magnificent. She took me in her arms and stroked my forehead. "Happy birthday, my little Marie." And with a sob, I dislodged the stone that was crushing my heart and felt a mother's care-worn hands stroking my face.[19]

Marie relived happy memories, savoring them:

> I relive them, and then I move on to

something else. I go for a walk, I sit down in the lobby, I go down to the activities room. I watch, I listen; my heart beats. It seems to me that I am learning how to live. It is high time, for I am old enough to have done with it . . . and young enough to begin again. If I told anyone that, they would regard me as mad. Because I am becoming wise?

The important thing for a candle is not where it is placed; it is the light that shines out from it, right to the end.[20]

According to Marie, if we become radiant old people, it doesn't matter where we end our lives.

## A Humanist Solution

I went to spend a day at the Villa Épidaure, a beautiful home at La Celle-Saint-Cloud, in the western suburbs of Paris, that houses eighty-four patients suffering from Alzheimer's disease. The architecture has been carefully thought out, so as not to give the impression of a large establishment, but rather a family guesthouse. There are seven units of twelve patients, which resemble little kibbutzim, with a house mother in charge of each one.

The establishment's philosophy is profoundly humanist. The teams constantly think about how they can respect the residents' dignity and listen to their families, for it is the families who suffer the most. I took part in one of the discussion groups where relatives come to express their difficulties and their feelings. It becomes painful when their relative enters the final phase of the illness, which sometimes lasts a very long time. Those readers who have experienced this situation will know how it feels to pay visit after visit to a relative who no longer recognizes you at all. It becomes surreal. And as the situation drags on, you ask yourself a thousand questions. What meaning does it have? Why keep a person alive when communication is not possible anymore? Some families are crushed by the cost of this responsibility. They become aggressive. Particularly grave ethical problems arise. For, without a doubt, 90 percent of these patients would not have wished to live through this.

A word about the legal implications of this kind of care: in France, a law on "Patients' Rights and the End of Life" was passed in 2005 allowing that advanced directives be made to stop treatment under specific circumstances, without permitting euthanasia. In the United States, powers of attorney and living wills can be made, but they are subject to the laws of the state. While physicians may assist in the termination of life to comply with patients' demands in France, this is often a chargeable offense in the United States. Ultimately certain decisions will always remain difficult. For example, should one administer an antibiotic when a patient who has reached the third stage of the illness develops pneumonia? Should a person who refuses to eat be fed through a gastric tube?

Limiting or halting treatment always poses the question of how one knows the correct course of action. The families, like the caregivers, have ambivalent attitudes, and this highlights the dissensions, the disharmony. Children who had a good relationship with their parent can more easily accept his or her decline and death. This is not the case with those who had a stormy relationship.

Recent French legislation obliges teams to think in a new way about what is now known as "allowing a patient to die." This is an attitude that is not automatic for caregivers, especially when — as is often the case — they are emotionally attached to a patient.

I met the wife of a patient who had reached the last stage of Alzheimer's. She told me about the development of her husband's illness, from the poignant silence with which he greeted the diagnosis to the mood swings and aggression — signs that he was ill. Although they were very close, he never shared his torment with her. When the psychiatrist who was treating her husband explained that he would have to be transferred to a specialized institute, he closed his eyes and did not reopen them again before his departure. After that, he seemingly built up a wall around himself. His wife told me: "He never asked to see the house again."

For her, this separation was very hard, for they had never been apart. At the start, she came every day to see him; they listened to music, and she took him out for walks. And then tendinitis obliged her to space out her visits. Eventually, she thought that he no longer recognized her, but he was still as sensitive as ever and sometimes had tears in his eyes when he listened to music. She continued to come, out of loyalty. What reassured her was that from the very beginning of his time at the Villa Épidaure, he trusted the staff to take care of him. Thousands of people, like this woman, suffer helplessly while watching a loved one decline. And yet they remain with that loved one right to the end.

Among the fears I mentioned at the beginning of this chapter, the most widespread is the fear of ending our lives suffering from dementia and imposing the burden of this illness upon those around us. Clearly, each of us hopes to be spared this fate. I have thought about what might help me to cope with this illness if I or one of my relatives were to be struck by it one day. Knowing that humane establishments like the one I just mentioned exist does me good.

## Seeing Dementia Differently

Laurence Serfaty's documentary *Alzheimer jusqu'au bout de la vie* (Alzheimer's to the End of Life), which was filmed in Quebec, recounts daily life in a pilot residence, the Carpe Diem home. He documented images that may alter our very pessimistic view of this illness. Although the patients there are slipping progressively into darkness, the carers are eager to see "what still works" in them. One senses that they are fond of their patients, and they reject any standardized care procedures in favor of adaptation to each individual. Consequently, as we watch this film, we begin to believe that it is possible to end one's life with dignity and integrity intact even if one has fallen victim to this illness that people fear so greatly, and that it is possible to communicate with a dementia sufferer as long as we maintain a link with him. We must be convinced that it is worth the trouble, because the patient is still "a person and not the remains of a fallen human being who is forever out of reach."[21]

These examples assuage my fears that I may one day have to bring one of my own relatives to an institution of this type. As Christian Bobin put it so well: "Alzheimer's disease removes what a person's upbringing has instilled in them, and brings the heart back to the surface. They speak with their eyes, and what I read there enlightens me better than books. . . . When I return from a visit to the long-term home, I bring with me a need to touch the shoulders of those I meet, however fleetingly, and an increased contempt for fine words."[22]

What better way of saying that even the most vulnerable of our elderly people have something to pass on to us? If that is the case, we must try to combat the widespread belief that dementia sufferers have nothing left to contribute and that in their condition their lives are no longer lives at all.

The idea that even if I was suffering from dementia I could still contribute something to my loved ones is another thought that helps me to plan for the worst.

I recently received a letter from a woman my own age who said she had found meaning in her mother's illness. She told me that it had brought her something that she had been missing for a very long time. "At last I have the opportunity to cuddle her, to take her in my arms and show her my affection. She allows me to express what I have never before been able to do, as before her illness she was cold and used to push me away."

Alzheimer's disease remains a mystery. Theories circulate about possible environmental causes of the illness, such as loneliness. Support associations for the families of Alzheimer's sufferers feel they are under attack from the loneliness hypothesis and prefer the biogenesis explanation, which doesn't imply that they are culpable. I think we should avoid being Manichaean. It is certainly an illness with many factors; other, admittedly less widespread theories circulate regarding causes that are psychological or linked to life events. The psychiatrist Jean Maisondieu has no hesitation in suggesting that Alzheimer's may be "a cry, a refusal, a sort of social and intellectual suicide."[23] Why has this person decided to be dead before their death, to withdraw from life?

He suggests that they do it so as not to see themselves growing old.

Aude Zeller, a psychotherapist, published a book about her mother's six-year decline.[24] Writing about the physical and mental degeneration of people affected by Alzheimer's disease is relatively rare. It is a taboo subject. But the way Aude Zeller examines this painful reality is so profound and so new that it deserves a mention here. Senile dementia is apparently not solely the simple destruction of an individual's mental and psychic abilities. What appears from outside to be a regression could also be the opportunity for a slow and final transformation.

This is an original thesis, and one that can help us a great deal. When degeneration makes the deficient elderly person regress to a state of dependence similar to that of a very small child, this enables him or her to return to a form of mental organization wherein the fear of death does not yet exist. So it is a way of preparing oneself for death. Understanding that this regression is potentially meaningful, and not simply absurd, may enable those around the patient to give psychological support.

Aude's account of the dizzying fall into dementia — what her mother calls her "unpicking" — expresses a sense of the progressive and implacable loss of everything that had contributed to her mother's identity as a woman: the loss of sight, hearing, and speech, but also the loss of control of her hand movements and therefore her self-sufficiency. "When you can no longer pick up a glass to drink or a fork to eat, nor scratch your nose just for the fun of it, your relationship to your body flounders in the muddy, sticky bog of total dependency."[25] The loss of power over others, and the loss of all self-control, leads to savage outpourings of language that are aggressive, sometimes obscene, and most of the time delirious. The return of the repressed — that is what Aude Zeller calls these rants, amid which it is very difficult to recognize her mother.

She does, however, try to understand what is happening. In the past, her mother did not feel she had permission to lay bare her secret desires. There is a whole sexual vitality that was kept under lock and key, and she is now attempting to free herself from her former moral shackles. "The delirious episodes that escaped from her lips centered on the vast theme of wrongs done to her female sensitivity. There was therefore a meaning, despite the painful effects. It was healthy not to contradict her but to listen."[26]

Contrary to appearances, Aude Zeller tells us, the dementia sufferer has a certain diffuse awareness of the way she is distorting reality. It would be a major, disrespectful mistake to behave as if nothing were wrong. For the ravings represent "a desperate reaching toward what is ample, vast, broad," from which the dementia sufferer feels set apart due to the penalties of old age.

But when almost everything has been lost, what truly matters still remains. "A year and a half before her death, when I had just read her a psalm from her Bible and we were both asking for God's blessing in accordance with her old customs and her spiritual life, to my great astonishment she raised her tear-filled eyes and responded, 'That hasn't been unpicked from me yet.' "[27]

Many of my colleagues who are psychotherapists start from the hypothesis that Alzheimer's disease is a progressive way to avoid confronting the approach of death.

One story supports this hypothesis. The man who told it to me is almost sixty. He lives in Madagascar and comes to France every six months to see his children and, especially, his old father, who is an inpatient in an establishment for Alzheimer's sufferers. His father has reached the final stage of the disease and no longer recognizes his son. At the end of his tether, the son asked him just before Christmas: "Father, why are you still here? What is there left for you to do in this life?" It was a tough question to ask, for it is utterly taboo to tackle the question of death. It was then that his father looked him straight in the eye and answered: "It's not an easy step to take!" It was a straight answer to a straight question.

I have always thought that if the loved ones of dementia patients told them the truth, they would obtain responses that show that not every trace of awareness has been extinguished.

Should I lapse into dementia, I have asked my children to respect my wish not to be kept alive beyond the stage where I no longer recognize them. I have asked them to tell me the truth, to talk to me as if I were fully aware, as my friend from Madagascar did. For I am personally convinced that "something" inside me, no doubt buried deep in my subconscious, will still hear what they are saying to me. I am reassured by the thought that the new French law on patients' rights and the end of life strengthens my right to refuse treatments that would force me to live, and asks the doctors to take into account my prior instructions.

If all the right conditions are present — a humane establishment, children who talk to me in the language of truth, and doctors who respect my wish not to continue to live beyond a certain stage — it seems to me that the prospect of having to end my life stricken with Alzheimer's disease would be less painful. It is even less so if, as I sense, the process of self-completion continues deep inside.

## The Right Kind of Care

As we have seen from these examples, the human dimension can be present wherever we end our lives. It is this dimension that we must defend in a world that is sometimes overly technical, one in which we forget that we are dealing with people. We have every reason to think that the humanity and dignity we would want for ourselves and for our loved ones will continue to grow, as the authorities have gauged the extent of mis-treatment and taken steps to humanize the end of life for elderly persons in residential care.

If we wish to enable elderly people to continue to be "human individuals" right to the end, we must treat them with respect, attention, and affection, just as we do with newborns. Carers must be taught to question all the technical skills they have learned that do not include tenderness or compassion. First, they must unlearn the tendency to treat the aged person as an object, something that is handled without respect, and they must acquire a different approach, one that is full of humanity. Although an ordinary patient can, in a pinch, accept being handled like a thing because it is useful or necessary, it is easy to comprehend that a very vulnerable person, or one suffering from dementia, cannot tell the difference between a touch that is objectifying and one that is aggressive. If we touch such a patient, it must be done gently and with kindness. Training programs exist that teach a methodology based on relationships, compassion, and touch.[28]

The "philosophy of humanitude" and the Gineste-Marescotti method in particular place the human bond at the center of care. In France, more and more retirement homes are moving to this type of training, and the results are clear: agitated behavior among residents has diminished considerably, and there is much less turnover among the carers.

The mainstays of the Gineste-Marescotti method are looking, talking, and touching.

People habitually fail to really look at the elderly. Carers need to realize that they often do not look at the person they are caring for but avoid the patient's gaze by looking up, into the distance, or aslant before turning away to get on with their work. Instead, they are taught to position themselves at the level of the patient's face, meeting his or her gaze, with no hesitation in getting as close as a few centimeters. When carers are not afraid to look directly into the other person's eyes, surprising changes have been witnessed. People emerge from their dark night. It is easy to appreciate the importance of speech, of affectionate words, when we consider that a bedridden old man who is disoriented and withdrawn is spoken to for an average of only 120 seconds per day. Old people are seldom touched with tenderness. Often the carers are not aware of how rough and swift their movements are; they have no concept of the aggression this represents to the very vulnerable patient. In a humane training program, carers learn gestures that are all-enveloping, affectionate, reassuring, and much more effective because they relax bodies.

This is how Florence Deguen, a journalist, described one of the most moving scenes in a 2006 film shot in a retirement home:

This film is the secret weapon of the Gineste-Marescotti training institute. It lasts roughly ten minutes and provokes tears, so clearly does it illustrate the miracles that can be achieved with a little humanitude. . . . Jeanne is an old lady of eighty-five who has not moved from her bed for a year and a half. Her eyes are almost always closed, her knees drawn up in the fetal position, she no longer reacts to anything, and she is force-fed . . . until a care assistant trained in humanitude comes to coax her from the depths of her bed. For three long minutes, the young woman works doggedly but without success, using a soft voice and making sure that her face is on a level with the old lady's closed mask. "Please, Jeanne, I'm a friend, open your eyes . . ." Jeanne resists, immured in her alarming fixedness. The care assistant strokes her shoulder, and calls to her again and again; and then suddenly Jeanne's eyelids flutter, hesitate, and open. It is not yet a human gaze, just two vague eyes, surprised that they have been coaxed out of their lethargy. They have difficulty focusing, and take a few seconds to meet the care assistant's gaze directly; but from that moment on,

Jeanne gently comes back to life . . . sits up in her bed, allows herself to be washed, consents to eat sitting up, utters her first yes and no for a year and a half, and even walks again . . . before telling the care assistant in a breath, "I love you."[29]

What I read did not surprise me. I have witnessed similar miracles worked by Julie and Simone, the care assistants in the palliative-care unit where I worked as a psychologist, and I have seen people who were no more than ghosts come back to life. Of course, this technique assumes that one puts one's heart into it, but it also demands an ability to establish what is known as "the correct distance."

This does not mean that one must harden oneself in order to protect oneself from the relationship. On the contrary, one must remain sensitive to the other person's emotions and not confuse them with one's own. Neutrality in emotions is illusory and prevents a caregiver from remaining a human being.

One thing is certain: when carers learn to be affectionate, they regain a degree of self-esteem and become less exhausted, and they discover that their work can give them pleasure.

It is not a question of blaming them for doing wrong. They simply received a training so strongly based on health education and ergonomics that they forgot they were also there to help the patient. What we must do is value qualities that have not been prized in the past, such as gentleness, touch, and presence, and encourage carers to display a humane approach in front of their colleagues.

The argument that there is a shortage of time and staff in aged-care establishments is often trotted out erroneously as an excuse for an absence of humanity. Being humane does not take more time. On the contrary, when you are truly there for the other person, you discover that you can do the same thing but better, and in the same amount of time. For too long, some carers felt that they were criticized simply for being compassionate, so they hid their gestures of affection. This is not acceptable. It is evidence that in addition to training carers to work in this way, health officials and nursing home managers have accepted this way of behaving. What is needed is a common culture of humanity in service, and an acceptance of collective responsibility. The effort will be worth it. In an age when we complain that we cannot recruit enough carers and care assistants to work in retirement homes and hospitals for the dependent elderly, we should consider the attractiveness of a humane training program for those interested in working in these establishments.

The benefits of an approach that respects the pace of life and the sensitivity and dignity of the elderly are obvious. When this approach is taken, many problems disappear — notably patient agitation, for example — and fewer tranquilizers are prescribed. Some geriatricians also report that their patients are slower to become bedridden.

# Encounters with Remarkable Elderly People

By this point in my research, I was convinced that if we could surround ourselves with goodwill and keep our hearts open and a ray of light shining deep within us, our old age, whatever it might be like, would have dignity and meaning. With such an approach, the place where we lived would undoubtedly be less important than we might imagine. I felt I was ready at last to return to those wise words of Olivier de Ladoucette, who insists that we can experience advancing age as a victory. Shortly after my meeting with him, I read a magazine containing "ten testimonies by magnificent senior citizens," and this reassured me.[1]

In the magazine, the feminist writer Benoîte Groult declares: "What age gives you is youthfulness of heart." Later on she complains about experiencing a stage of life where so much time is spent saying "Ouch!" She goes on: "To be able to open one's shutters each morning, and discover the newborn day . . . and the world becomes fresh again. Whereas when you're young, you just open the shutters mechanically. . . . Each gesture acquires value, and you become curious about everything, much more curious than before. For example, I have just discovered poetry, which encourages you to think, brings you back to what really matters. I am discovering the great value of motionless journeys. When I was moving around, I neglected this, but now I savor it."

Singer Henri Salvador takes these ideas further: "This curiosity is what preserves you. It's the antiaging drug par excellence." Like so many others, he reminds us that the key to happiness consists of savoring the present moment, the good times, for "Life is fabulous! Anyone would think that people don't realize; they complain all the time, groan, whine, revel in their misfortunes. I see only the good moments; the others, I forget." Similarly, in the same magazine I read that the oldest member of the French Senate, Paulette Brisepierre, has declared that the older she gets, the more fantastic she finds life.

At the age of seventy-nine, choreographer Maurice Béjart says that growing old does not damage the creative impulse; while he is no longer able to dance, he experiences dance through his students. Denise Desjardins, aged eighty-three, writes that in India people believe that something continues to grow within us right to the end; they talk of one's "inner lord." "It is also called the Self, the 'true being,' all kinds of names that express something permanent, immovable, almost eternal." At the age of almost ninety, publisher Robert Laffont speaks of the "joy of contemplating his life inside out."[2] Although his body may feel old and heavy, his mind feels increasingly light, relaxed, and serene. He is still learning from life, notably how to "resonate and commune with the world" that surrounds him. Writer Claude Sarraute, aged eighty, talks about a very pleasant kind of freedom for a woman: not feeling obliged to be sexy! She is less dependent upon the way others see her, and feels that she can say what she wants without the fear of being judged. Philologist Jacqueline de Romilly, aged ninety-three, also confirms that the mind remains young and that one can finally leave one's "little me" and "ascend toward wisdom." Last, for Professor Etienne-Emile Baulieu, it is essential to make room for pleasure, voluptuousness, and sensuality in order to experience a happy old age.

Reading through the perspectives of these magnificent senior citizens prompted me to talk to two people whom I love and who, each in their own way, make me want to grow old. Being with them does me so much good that I think of them as my good-luck charms. So here they are. They are both well-known media figures in France, and both are radiant elderly people.

The first is Sister Emmanuelle.[3] At almost one hundred years of age, this nun is known to all French people for her charisma and the twenty years she spent working in the shanty towns of Cairo, combating poverty and illiteracy. She has constantly helped those of her contemporaries who are "pursued by nonsense" and are in search of spiritual liberation.

Sister Emmanuelle is very media-friendly, and in French popularity polls she is up there with pop singer Johnny Hallyday. She has used this popularity to preach the way of the heart, constantly and tirelessly. Well aware of the personal enjoyment she has derived from being in the media spotlight, she has finally come to a clear-headed acceptance of it. "I realized," she says, "that it is impossible to separate the hard kernel of self-interest from the breath of love for others."[4] What better way is there of saying that there is no such thing as a totally selfless act? "Our nature seeks to blossom. It contains within itself the thirst for pleasure, for possession, for pride, just as it also contains the impulse to give, to serve, and to be compassionate."[5] I am touched by the humility and the truth that Sister Emmanuelle displays in talking about herself in this way. This woman is real, and that is why I went to see her in order to hear her story.

It was late in the afternoon when she greeted me, seated in her armchair in the Deaconesses' hospital in Versailles. She has been a resident there since an illness struck her down when she was about to deliver an address in northern France. She is stooped and lined, but her eyes are still incredibly lively, her voice is still strong, and her mind is as alert as ever. Although she is almost one hundred years old, I cannot stop myself from thinking: What youthfulness! What energy!

We have known each other for several years. The first time I heard her speak was at Aix-les-Bains, during a large forum devoted to the subject of love, where she talked to us about the French philosopher Henri Bergson. Standing there in her rather unflattering nun's habit, she looked extremely frail, and yet she was luminous. Brandishing a dead leaf, she talked to us about the human heart, comparing it to an immense, deep lake covered with dead leaves: the leaves of sadness and bitterness. It is absolutely vital, she said, to break through this bark of sadness and dive into the depths of the lake — that is to say, into the depths of the heart. We must have the courage to explore our own depths, to draw upon them, she repeated, as though imparting something of her immense faith in mankind. "Man surpasses man," she recalled, quoting Pascal, her favorite philosopher. It was Pascal who taught her about "man's greatness of thought."[6]

We met up again a few months later when I was presented with the Légion d'honneur, an honor conferred by the French government. I requested that she be the one to present me with the insignia at the awards ceremony, as I wanted this distinction to be awarded to me by someone profoundly committed to serving humanity. She agreed to do it because she had much enjoyed my book *Intimate Death*, and the ceremony forged a bond between us.

Now, in her hospital room, she admitted that she felt vulnerable. Her illness was like a sign showing her that death might not be very far away now, and she told me that she thought about it every day, but without a trace of fear. She was ready. "For me, it's like a child falling into the arms of her father," she told me as she talked about death.

I had come to ask her to share something of her experience of growing old. Her testimony is certainly not representative of what the majority of our elderly people experience, for Sister Emmanuelle is a sort of saint, and I could be criticized for seeking out examples of people one cannot identify with. And although I was aware of this, I went to see her anyway, for I believe that we need the words of those who raise us up. I hope that each reader will take something that helps him or her to move forward into old age from the words that follow.

When I invited Sister Emmanuelle to talk to me about her old age, she looked me straight in the eye.

"Well, you see, Marie, old age is the most beautiful period of my life. I feel as though I am rich from all the encounters I have experienced. Thousands and thousands of people have enriched me, so I have an immense store of capital, and feel responsible for passing on what I have received."

When I pointed out to her that people view her as a wise woman, she retorted:

"But I am not wise, Marie! I am a bit of a crank! I launch myself into adventures, and I'm unreasonable; I've always been like that. I always did whatever I did, come hell or high water, though nobody approved. When I became a nun, everyone laughed at me, because I was a girl who enjoyed having fun, traveling, and dancing with good-looking boys. I was a flirt. Looking good was important to me. So people said to me: 'What on earth are you going to do in a convent?' The others didn't see that deep down in my heart, I had a desire for the absolute. I flirted, and I traveled, but where was that leading me? I felt that I was made for something that doesn't pass away. I wasn't then familiar with the words of Pascal: 'Everything slips away from us and flees with an eternal flight.' I sensed that everything was slipping out of my hands, and I wanted what doesn't pass away: love, love that is free and true, for that is eternal."

A few years ago, when she and I discussed our respective childhoods, Sister Emmanuelle told me what a determining moment it had been for her when, at the age of four, she saw her father drown right in front of her. I reminded her of our conversation.

"That day, you realized, deep inside you, that everything passes away, that life is transient. You did indeed search for something that doesn't pass away."

"Yes. I realized that if I loved a man, if I got married, that man would die one day, as I had seen my father die. I had to have an absolute love, a love that would not die. I have never regretted choosing the religious life; it has freed me. When I traded my little flirty girl's dress for the austere novice's habit, a black robe that hung down to my feet, and a little veil on my head attached by two completely ridiculous strings, I looked like a widow — but I didn't mind because I was free! I was free! I had taken a vow of poverty, so I no longer needed money; I had taken a vow of chastity, so good-looking boys no longer interested me; I had taken a vow of obedience; and I had a superior with whom I was going to seek out the right path. In short, I was free! And I still feel free, perhaps even more so now."

"So you would say that old age confers even greater freedom?" I asked.

"Yes, I think so. Contacts are so much easier, and the affection that may seem ambiguous when one is younger, and which consequently one may not dare to experience fully, becomes a very clear human dimension. I have very affectionate friendships, which are real and which give me a great deal. And also, when I see my life unfolding, I feel at peace. I made the right choices."

I then asked her how she spends all her days. She replied:

"I have visits from friends, people from the association that I founded and whose activities I follow closely. I don't know why, but I have an enormous number of young friends, and I rediscover myself in them. Young people refresh my soul; it's delicious! One can be old and still have a young heart; it's a marvel. As I've grown older, I have become extremely sensitive. Respect and affection do me good. Before, I did not feel the need to be surrounded by smiles and kindness. Now I enjoy it very much, and it helps me not to be an old grouch!"

Did she sometimes feel lonely?

"Never! You see, Marie, I believe deeply in the presence of a spirit of love that dwells within us. It is my home. I enjoy it constantly."

"Do you call this presence God?" I ventured.

Her face lit up; suddenly, it was the face of a young girl.

"I have two infinite sources of joy: God and mankind. I believe in God, and I believe in mankind. When I am alone, I pray. I always have my rosary within reach. I take into my prayers all the people who are in my heart, and I make an immense bouquet that I offer up from morning till night. 'Lord, please bless all those I love!' I am sure that God is listening to me, that He helps them to bear their lives, to surmount obstacles, to love."

When I asked her what she would like to say to all those who are entering the third age and who are afraid of growing old, she concluded in a voice that was strikingly firm and gentle:

"Do not be afraid! Old age is like a coronation. I have reached the summit of my life, and I see the world and other people with infinite tenderness. I feel them in my heart. This affectionate contemplation gives me immense joy. For me, it is like champagne! Joy bursts forth in my heart!

"You, too, can dispense this joy around you. One becomes old the day one no longer believes in mankind and in the worth of every individual, whoever he or she may be. Take these words of a Muslim poet who I am very fond of and make them yours: 'Break open the heart of man and there you will find a sun!' But in order to do that, you must forget yourself a little, and take an interest in others!

"Elderly people should realize that it is their mission to love. Whatever the state in which one grows old, one can look, smile, stretch out one's hand, and bless. And that transfigures life."

It is faith and love that light up old age, and Sister Emmanuelle is an example of that. Her faith is rooted in her religious experience; other radiant elderly people, as we shall see, are borne along not by a religious faith but quite simply by a faith in life and in mankind.

That is the case with my friend Stéphane Hessel, who is a great humanist, a man of commitment and dialogue. A former Resistance member who was deported during World War II, Stéphane subsequently became a French diplomat at the United Nations. He is a member of the international ethical, scientific, and political collegium created by Michel Rocard; as such, he travels the world to deliver lectures and so defend what he calls the culture of peace. His most recent book on social democracy has become a best seller around the world.

He defines himself as a sort of gardener.

"Cultivating peace means cultivating understanding, dialogue, and communication, not violence," he repeats tirelessly.

I took advantage of the friendship that binds us to ask him to offer a few thoughts on old age. What were his experiences of this period in his life?

Readers should know that Stéphane Hessel is ninety years old. He is a slender, elegant man in good health, but he is above all a man of great culture who one senses is filled with an infectious joie de vivre and happiness. In his eyes, and through his broad smile, one can see the light of which Victor Hugo speaks.[7]

"Where do this youthfulness and light come from?" I asked.

"They come to me from my mother, Hélène. When I was little, one of my mother's favorite sayings was: 'Let's vow to be happy!' She used to tell me that the best thing any of us can do is to experience and plan for happiness. One can also plan one's sufferings, one's pain, but there's no point in that. The first years of life see the formation of a psyche, whose ability to be radiant can be strengthened. I had the good fortune to be initiated into happiness and, subsequently, I have cultivated happiness all my life.

"I am well aware of the fact that this has led me to construct myself in the image of a friendly person. I need to be liked. The other side of the coin is that I have such a desire to appear to be someone who is listening, positive, and constructive that I have a great deal of difficulty in defending myself when people don't agree with me or attack me. My tendency is to try to understand, not to retaliate vigorously; and also, when someone asks me to do something, I can't say no.

"Besides this feeling of happiness, which I get from my mother, I feel that I have been lucky in my life. There have been at least four times when I have rubbed shoulders very closely with death, and survived. I call that luck. When one has a lot of bad luck, it is more difficult to grow old positively. I say to my friends: 'You have to encounter death at least once in your life.' It's an important experience. Life is a possession, and one runs the risk of forgetting that if it hasn't been saved at a moment when one might have lost it. This applies to wartime, but also to serious illness."

Stéphane knows what he is talking about. After enlisting in the forces of General de Gaulle, he was arrested in 1944, deported to Buchenwald, and then to Dora, where he would undoubtedly have died if he had not benefited from a piece of unexpected good luck. One night, someone came to alert him that preparations for an escape attempt were under way. One of the participants had just died, so there was a spare place, and it was offered to him. Stéphane escaped with some others that night. Knowing this, one can better understand this man's feeling of gratitude for the simple fact of being alive. But how does he maintain this joie de vivre?

Stéphane has always loved poetry. For as long as he can remember, he has learned and recited the poems he loves, and every dinner involving him is bound to end with the recitation of one or two poems, in French or in English. Evenings with him have a tremendous charm, for one can sense that he is entirely in the poem, in its rhythm, in the emotion it arouses. You listen to him with closed eyes, and follow the inflections of his voice, which are sometimes imperceptible in the moments that touch the soul most deeply. I must confess that one feels transported.

Apart from the fact that it is excellent for the memory to recite a poem a day, for this man who loves life and is immensely grateful for it, this daily practice is a sort of prayer.

For his eighty-eighth birthday, Stéphane edited an anthology.[8] He chose eighty-eight poems on the subject of death, and shared with the reader the emotions that these texts aroused in him.

"I would like to reintroduce the idea of death to people," he told me. "You see, one of my trump cards is that I have a very positive attitude about it. I want to die. Not tomorrow, or the day after that, but I very much want my life to reach its culmination, and I would like that culmination to happen before I have lost too much of my strength. Of course, one does grow weaker, but if one could just say to oneself, as many people do: 'Right, that's that, my life has been marvelous. I shall leave it with all the more pleasure, knowing that I still enjoy living and will therefore enjoy dying, for to me the two pleasures are but one.' . . . I very much believe that death is merely a transition, like birth. Something in us is widely scattered in time.

"If one can have this positive attitude with regard to death, one can avoid being afraid of growing old, knowing that one will find the means to let go when the time seems to have come. I agree that these considerations don't really hold water, for we don't yet really have the means to say: 'Off we go, then! This is where I stop.' Why now? Because I'm about to turn ninety? It may seem absurd, presenting myself with such a hurdle!

"I am in favor of giving people the opportunity to decide that they have had enough, and find a 'friendly' way of ending things. But how can this choice to end life be respected without resorting to euthanasia, without asking someone else to get involved in your death?"

Stéphane then related how his mother-in-law, his second wife's mother, died at the age of eighty-nine. "She said that she wanted to go. She didn't do anything in particular, or anything very active, like refusing food. She just let death take her. And death came. I think that one can summon death."

So one can summon one's own death! Stéphane thinks so. As he has grown older, his belief in the "invisible" has grown.

He then told me about an admirable work by Rilke that he had discovered and which he had just translated. In it, Rilke is replying to a friend who tells him that he wishes he could understand *The Duino Elegies*. In this beautiful seven-page letter, Stéphane tells me, Rilke writes: "What I have discovered is that life is surrounded by the Invisible, that the angels live in this invisible world, and that our task as men is to transform the visible into Invisible. We are bees, which gather the gold of the visible world in order to create the framework of the Invisible." This text indicates that the fact that we are mortal gives us permission to extract the substance from life and give it bodily form inside us, so that it crosses earthly boundaries. Naturally, poetry is one of the elements that bring us closer to the angels.

"Our task," Rilke writes, "is to imprint this temporary, outmoded earth inside ourselves so profoundly, so painfully, and so passionately that its essence wells up again within us, invisibly. We are the bees of invisibility. We frantically gather honey from the visible world in order to store it up in the great golden hive of the Invisible."

I then asked Stéphane why this text by Rilke touched him so deeply. He told me that it sums up marvelously the mission with which each of us has been entrusted. Human beings are capable of determining the species' destiny. Over the last century, the human species has acquired an immense standing. "It has a new capacity for existence," said Stéphane. "What it has discovered about itself since Freud and Einstein, this transformation, implies a responsibility.

Man is responsible for man. He cannot behave just any way."

Now, is it not up to all elderly people, all future centenarians, to remind the coming generations, those who are just beginning their lives, of everything they have learned both about the world and about mankind? We who have experienced war now know that the human race is capable of the worst barbarity, but it is also capable of organizing itself according to great principles like the Declaration of the Rights of Man, and of ensuring that they are respected. Stéphane continued: "We know now that war is never victorious, that violence is not the solution. We know which paths lead to peace, to development and democracy: dialogue, listening, negotiation. We know that if we do not tread those paths, we shall run enormous risks.

"When we returned from the camps, we were not questioned; nobody asked us what this experience had taught us. Today, on the sixtieth anniversary of the liberation of the camps, people are asking us questions. The director of the Buchenwald Memorial invited seventy young people from all over Europe and asked them to interview a survivor of the camps. The young people asked us some interesting questions, then they presented a sketch incorporating every-thing that had made an impression upon them. They had indeed retained something: not only the misery, the degradation, and the pain, but also the taste for life, the desire to be useful, which the survivors wished to pass on."

So, here we have two individuals who have reached a great age. Each is very different from the other. One is a believer; the other is not. One has lived alone in a community; the other has been married twice and has several children and grandchildren. Their paths have also been different, but what they have in common are a very strong commit-ment to their life choices, vitality, optimism, a faith in life in the face of all ordeals, and a capacity for joy and wonderment. What meaning do they attribute to this last stage in their lives? They see it as an opportunity to continue enriching themselves emotion-ally and spiritually, and to pass on their experience, their values, and their faith in mankind to younger generations.

Having met them, we now know that it is possible to live to old age and retain our self-esteem, experience moments of joy and happiness, and continue to learn from life.

But how can we achieve this? How can we experience such a fulfilling old age?

# Keys to a Happy Old Age

Our generation will have longer and better lives. Our responsibility is not only to "grow old well" but also to turn this experience into something good and happy — an enviable adventure.

It is true that we are not all equal when we enter into this adventure. Those who have made life choices that have not damaged them too much will enter this "new age" differently from those who have burned their candles at both ends, so to speak. In these later years, we will pay for past mistakes and negligence.

In France, the authorities have decided to devote large sums of money to an "Aging Well" plan, doubtlessly because they are aware of this inequality vis-à-vis growing old.[1] Tomorrow's young pensioners will be able to take stock of their financial circumstances and their state of health, and will have access to information on how to grow old successfully in terms of nutrition and physical activity. This Aging Well plan is already attracting severe criticism. Some people feel that it will emphasize the division between wealthy and poor pensioners. Not everyone has the means to maintain a rewarding social life for as long as possible, to make regular physical and sporting activity a priority, or to have a healthy and varied diet. This is as true in the United States as it is in France.

However, we don't just confront the challenge of aging well by means of a good diet, a balanced lifestyle, sports, and sleep. Our state of mind will also contribute significantly. As it was written in a Roman text dating back more than two thousand years: "It is not enough to pay attention to one's body; one must also take care of the mind and soul. Both, indeed, run the risk of being extinguished by old age like the flame of a lamp deprived of oil."[2] Unfortunately, the official Aging Well plan completely overlooks the psychological and spiritual dimensions of growing old. No suggestions are given to help our generation make the profound changes that would enable us to embark upon old age serenely, and without a key there can be no strategy. Perhaps the authorities feel that this realm belongs exclusively to each individual's private life. Later, we shall see that the philosopher Robert Misrahi advocates education as a means of learning how to grow old well. According to him, this should come under the heading of "public health."

## Strategies That Work

In the book *Rester jeune, c'est dans la tête* (Staying Young Is All in the Mind), Olivier de Ladoucette devotes a chapter to the psychological strategies that can enable an individual to remain young. First, one should approach life in such a way as to combat stress. In particular, he cites studies from the United States that show that any traumatic event causes *"un coup de vieux,"* an attack of old age. "Two major sources of stress in a year make a person age sixteen years. In fact, an annus horribilis including three very serious events could increase the body's age by . . . thirty-two years, over the subsequent twelve months."[3]

He reminds us that "centenarians teach us that it is impossible to economize on good management of the emotions if we wish to live for a long time, in good health." Olivier de Ladoucette tells us that the biographer of Jeanne Calment, who died at the age of 122, was impressed by her ability to face up to adversity. She was, according to him, immunized against stress. She liked to repeat to anyone who would listen: "There is no such thing as an insurmountable ordeal; all you have to do each time is find a solution."[4]

What should we do in order to follow in Jeanne Calment's footsteps? Apart from the rules for a healthy lifestyle, which I have dealt with elsewhere — sleep, a frugal and balanced diet, exercise, and avoidance of alcohol and tobacco — we must be able to do the following:

1. Adapt to changing situations, retaining confidence in our own resources;
2. Accept our limits with good humor;
3. Learn how to refuse what we don't want to do;
4. Ensure that our daily routine incorporates time devoted to doing what we enjoy, in peace.

If, in addition, we can share our worries with those close to us, then we are on the right path.

## Up with People

Studies show that elderly people who have retained a network of relationships — both family and friends — live longer than others. Giving and receiving, and showing generosity, all have positive effects. Conversely, relationship conflicts are a veritable poison, which can eat away at a person like rust.

According to Olivier de Ladoucette, "Centenarians are almost never lonely. They have loyal people close to them who bring them daily physical and psychological support. These relationships exist because of a clear charisma, which inspires respect and affection, and exerts a strong power of attraction on people."[5]

It is a question of finding a balance between accepting solitude and having a rich emotional life. Emotional independence is not easy to maintain when one feels lonely. Many elderly people transfer their social expectations onto younger people who cannot fulfill them because, after all, they have their own lives. The ideal is not to expect too much of others but simply to be receptive. Being nice is the key, according to Jean-Louis Servan-Schreiber: "It is up to us to behave so that people enjoy listening to us, meeting us, and communicating with us.

Let's mellow! Let's be receptive!

"Certain elderly people are very good at achieving this alchemy," he wrote. "It can be found in a look, a smile, a pleasant tone of voice on the telephone. They have an instinct for making themselves agreeable. They never complain, expect nothing, have their own network of relationships, and take care of their own physical health. It is no longer a question of trying to seduce, which isn't appropriate, but of remaining attractive, cultivating one's charm."[6]

Charm no longer comes from smoothness of skin or strength of muscle, but from the soul, as we saw in the case of actress Tsilla Chelton, who appeared on the television program devoted to aging. Charm comes from the capacity to take an interest in others and in the world, to look at life with confidence, wonderment, and gratitude. "It is necessary to leave behind one's egocentricity and enter the other person's world," Robert Misrahi declared.[7]

Robert Dilts, the author of numerous works on the subject of neurolinguistic programming, carried out a study of elderly people who had retained their vitality. He took an interest in the psychological processes that characterized these individuals: their beliefs, their spirituality, their ability to overcome the stress resulting from the changes imposed by growing old, and their capacity to establish a new life framework for themselves. "We have quite a precise idea of the image of the healthy ninety-year-old. It is a happy person who is adaptable and has a balanced life and harmonious social relationships. The question is: how does one become like that? It is not enough to say: 'Have a happy, balanced life!' We want to discover the psychological processes that are at work behind this way of living."[8]

Dilts wondered how those who attain an advanced age with their vitality intact face up to stressful situations. What are the beliefs they rely upon in order to control their state of health, and what are their strategies regarding illness? His goal was to identify a psychological model that could then be used to help people who want to grow old in a more positive fashion.

The study was conducted at Nijmegen, in Holland. An appeal was launched on the radio aimed at individuals aged over eighty who were in good health and active. Thirty people responded, and Robert Dilts selected four of them — two men and two women with very different personalities and social situations.

The first thing he noted was that the capacity for a happy, fit old age may sometimes be found in people whose history, personalities, beliefs, and life strategies are radically opposed. So he searched for the common points shared by the four participants he had selected.

He was initially struck by their openmindedness, their freethinking, and their tolerance. The fact that they had been in contact with a range of very different people during their childhoods certainly played a part in this openness. Also, all four emphasized the importance of being active, singing, and seeing the positive side of life and events, and they regarded life's trials as an opportunity to evolve rather than as a sign of failure. All four emphasized the vital role of humor.

When questioned about defining moments in their lives, they cited their marriages as being the biggest change and the loss of a partner as being the greatest ordeal. They had all succeeded in working through their bereavement by internalizing the presence of the deceased loved one, whose protecting spirit they could still feel. The thought of death did not particularly preoccupy them. They knew that their lives were limited, but they lived as if they still had all their time ahead of them, and their capacity to look to the future was remarkable. Whereas in our society, the majority of people their age live in the past and cannot manage to project themselves into the future, Robert Dilts pointed out that if his four models were capable of envisaging the future, it was because they were at peace with their pasts. Moreover, they insisted that they would not change a single moment in their lives, even if those lives had been punctuated by painful events.

Their beliefs and values differed, but they shared the feeling that they were linked to something that was greater than they were, and they were in harmony with themselves. Deep down, they were all true to themselves, to their history and culture.

As for old age, they saw it as an opportunity, a kind of liberation, with fewer cares and more time to devote themselves to what really interested them, with freedom of speech, greater self-confidence, and a greater openness. "Each of them believed that their age enabled them to do things they weren't able to do when they were young," wrote Dilts, giving us one key to growing old well.[9]

So how can we help elderly people through this experience of growing old? How can they be taught to grow old well, to remain active while accepting the natural course of things, to be pleasant, to remain true to themselves, to take an interest in others and continue to learn from them, to see the positive side of things, and to retain a sense of humor?

Can these things be taught? Some people think it is naïve to believe so, and that grumpy, selfish, depressive people — those who have spent their lives complaining and annoying others — will not change. As far as these people are concerned, old age will only make things worse. They belong to the group of old people we avoid. Growing old well, they say, cannot be learned, for one ages as one has lived, faithful to one's virtues or one's vices.

Personally, I think that as we grow old, we change, and not always for the worse. Even for people who have not loved life, something can happen to awaken them. The advance of age, with the ordeals and bereavements it implies, is the opportunity for a turnaround. In life, each crisis is the chance for change. The Chinese understood this well, for in their language the hexagram, which signifies crisis, has a double meaning: on the one hand, chaos; on the other, luck. As we grow older, we have every chance to lay aside our egos and turn toward others, though this entails working on oneself and nurturing the determination to accomplish this change. It helps to realize that being in harmony with oneself and others is the only way to maintain a network of friends and good relations with one's children.

I knew a depressive, unpleasant man of eighty who changed completely after spending time in an intensive care unit. He thought he was dying, and when he emerged from the unit after two months, those around him didn't recognize him! He confided that he had not realized how much his family loved him despite his impossible personality, and he made the decision never to complain again and to thank heaven every day for the joy of life. He has become a lovely old man. So let us take as our starting point the principle that it is not impossible to change, to transform oneself. If I did not think this was the case, I would not have written this book for my generation.

The majority of the senior citizens who surround me do not want to be among those men and women who allow themselves to be helped and carried, without giving anything of themselves in exchange. They dream of being attractive old people, having had their fill of days, as it is written in the Bible, happy to have made it through life's adventures, and happy to end their days peacefully, viewing the world with the benevolence one acquires when there is nothing left to lose, prove, or defend.

This happiness in growing old must be earned, and nobody can do it for us. It is a question of real work. We have bereavements to endure and questions to ask. This demands courage and heart, in the sense that I used that term at the start of this book — in other words, vitality and desire. Only then will we be open to learning new things.

What is emerging today is the idea that growing old can be taught. I would not be surprised if in the years to come, training courses or seminars will be developed aimed at helping senior citizens learn to age well, psychologically and spiritually.

Olivier de Ladoucette believes that elderly people should be educated, that we retain our ability to learn right to the end of our lives.

Take, for example, the ability to see the positive side of things. We now know that optimism prolongs life. One American study conducted over a period of twenty-three years among six hundred people showed that individuals who demonstrated a positive attitude at the start of the study lived, on average, seven years longer than their more negative counterparts.[10] It is evident that the body needs signals of hope if it is to recuperate, to adapt, and to remain fit. Olivier de Ladoucette thinks that optimism can be learned, even late in life. We can learn to be positive, to look at life's good side at the age of sixty, even if we didn't acquire this aptitude in childhood. We can learn to challenge our own negative thoughts and to have confidence in existence, though we must want to learn these things, and we must be willing to seek help.

Many methods exist to develop positive thinking and to change people's behavior, including the Coué method, a technique in which people repeat to themselves what they desire in the quest for fulfillment; positive visualization; hypnosis techniques; and neurolinguistic programming. In behavioral psychology, protocols that train people to be optimistic have proved effective, and therapies that develop individuals' "basic security" enable them to rely progressively upon their own internal resources (this is, notably, the case in communicating with a fetus through sensory stimulation).

But all these strategies, all these keys to a successful old age, are effective only if we accept that we will grow old, if we accept that transformation.

# ACCEPTING GROWING OLD

Acceptance of old age begins with coming to terms with it. Those who have entered old age have a litany of complaints, such as: "I feel limited," "I'm losing my strength," "I can no longer do what I did before," "My body is kaput," "I'm becoming invisible, men don't look at me anymore," "I'm getting tired," and "People make me feel like they can do without me."

This is how one woman, Yvonne, related her experiences. The first shock came upon her retirement at the age of sixty-five. The sudden freedom was difficult to cope with, and Yvonne quickly realized how reassuring she had found the constraints of work, with its strict timetables. As long as she had been working, she had been on track, heading toward clear goals. Then, all at once, she was faced with the challenge of how to occupy her newfound freedom. She realized that retiring from work meant leaving the place where things were happening, so she felt excluded from a world that had occupied an important place in her life. Yvonne belongs to a generation of people who are proud of working, of earning their living, and of being independent. Certainly she felt real satisfaction in receiving her pension, for which she had saved for years — but she also knew that she was being supported by the younger generations, and that made her feel uncomfortable. "The exchange that had been established between what I gave to society through my work and what it gave me back in the form of a salary was a source of equilibrium for me, and that had been broken," she said.

She found it hard to accept the transformation of certain values and had difficulty adapting to new technology, such as the computer, e-mail, and the Internet. This difficulty accentuated her feeling that she had fallen behind the times. She felt that the experience she had acquired in her life was no longer relevant to the realities of today, and she found that it was difficult or impossible to communicate with her grandchildren. "Of course, it has always been that way between generations," she conceded, "but the phenomenon is exacerbated by the speed at which changes occur these days and the interminable duration of old age."

Yvonne wondered how interested her grandchildren's generation would be in what she had to communicate: her life experiences, with all her failures, sufferings, successes, and losses. She wanted to testify to the dynamic of life, and to share all that she had learned through bereavement, such as an awareness of the value of life and love, and the importance of the present, because everything is ephemeral. "Perhaps the main thing we can pass on to our grandchildren," she said, "is to maintain our place in the chain of generations, and not to hesitate in making our voices heard."

It was very touching to hear her talk about this responsibility, which Yvonne herself has now accepted: she has decided to take preemptive action so that she will not be an expensive burden to her children. At the age of seventy, she entered a local sheltered-housing development — an arrangement that she says enables her to lead her life as she wishes, and gives her the benefits of community support and an administrative staff that is on hand to help her if the need arises. She had to wait three years to obtain a place in the housing development. "It seemed to me that this way, I was bringing relief to my children, who live a long way away and would know that I was being well looked after, night and day."

This choice implies that Yvonne has accepted becoming old. More than that, she is also thinking about the stages to come: "One day, I may have to leave this sheltered accommodation for a medically supervised establishment; one day, I will have to give up driving before I am a danger on the road. I will have to live life in accordance with my abilities, and also think, peacefully, about my death."

This testimony is permeated by a feeling of sadness, for a kind of depression accompanies the moment when one realizes that one has become "elderly." One day something — a sensation, a perception, or some more serious event — makes us feel irredeemably old. It could be any one of a number of things: the deepening of wrinkles, the loss of one's hair, the appearance of age spots on the skin, difficulty in climbing a stepladder or lacing up one's shoes, a loss of libido, the disappearance of desire in the eyes of others, or someone giving up their seat on the bus. In such a moment, we are forced into awareness, and we are plunged into a new way of perceiving our lives.

Looked at one way, it may indeed seem like a shipwreck. We may be tempted to behave as if we aren't growing older. We might continue to dress like younger people, ignore the loss of physical strength, or make light of our problems with memory, sight, and hearing. But this denial of aging does not help us to grow old in a positive way. There are some who become hypochondriacs, obsessed with their health, and who talk about nothing else. Others complain incessantly as they grow older, which obviously is unbearable for those around them. Still others regress, adopting infantile behaviors or withdrawing from the world.

But we can also grow old intelligently; we can accept what we cannot change, and look toward all that has yet to be discovered.

There is a beneficial kind of depression that marks this essential stage of life, required in order for us to mature and move on to something new. As with any grieving process, one experiences a state of sadness and withdrawal, but there is nothing pathological about this. It is a process of internalization, required to allow us to draw the bright, living powers of the soul from deep within ourselves. For desire is still there. Our life's energy pushes us ever forward, continuing to seek that which is new, and this process continues right up to the last day of our lives.

## Final Frontiers

Carl Gustav Jung conceived a model that can help us to understand the progression into old age. In the first half of his life, the individual must assert himself, construct himself, and realize his ambitions. Generally, he does this in ignorance of that which constructs him — that is, his innermost being — and he sometimes works to the detriment of his personal freedom. We then see that as he enters his third or fourth stage of life, as he bids the inevitable farewell to his youth, his physical powers, his role in society, and his performance at work, he may discover a new freedom and inner life for himself. These new resources facilitate growth and transformation. Certainly, everyone changes and matures throughout life, but the transformation that accompanies the final stretch of years is a form of completion. As Michel de M'Uzan said, it is a question of "putting oneself completely into the world before passing away."[1] This process may take several decades, or only a few days. Self-completion means realizing one's true nature, allowing one's Self — one's essential being — to manifest. Above

157

all, it is a work of awareness.

The second half of life has a spiritual goal. It is characterized by the process of individuation, during which the Me — which one could also call the external man — is sacrificed to the Self, the inner man. It is in fact the Me, the ego, the external man, who experiences this "descent," while the Self, on the other hand, continues to progress. Only people who experience this transformation can understand Saint Paul's words to the Corinthians: "While our outer man is wasting away, our inner man is renewed day by day."[2]

Having read the words of Sister Emmanuelle and Stéphane Hessel, we know that this is possible. When we say that old age is not a shipwreck but is instead a form of growth, we clearly are referring not to something that happens in the outside world but to an inner ripening. The true meaning of old age is not performance but maturity.

Many people live according to external constraints and maintain a "false self" — that is to say, a personality built on compromises that sometimes run counter to the true personality of the individual. They try to live through the "afternoon of life" according to the "morning rules," thus running the risk that they will spend the last years of their existence desperately clinging to old patterns and outmoded thinking. They become a rigid caricature of what they used to be. As Olivier de Ladoucette says, "The morning's truth will be the evening's error."[3]

We can easily understand the ontological and spiritual meaning of the inevitable depression that accompanies the aging process. It teaches us humility and wisdom. As in Saint John of the Cross's "dark night of the soul," we are witnessing the death of the egotistical part of ourselves. The outer person is damaged; it hurts, it is unacceptable, and it is humiliating. Our souls are shaken by trembling and pangs of anxiety. We have a right to this depression, writes Hermann Hesse: "It seems to me that we then have the right to feel and remain small in the face of this, like children who use tears and weakness to regain their equilibrium after a disturbing incident."[4]

Once we have made it through the depression, a hitherto unsuspected strength will manifest itself — for though biological aging may be unstoppable and the body continues to change, the inner person is neither damaged by nor concerned about growing old. We continue to evolve, to progress. But in order to accomplish this we must accept and subscribe to reality: no further compromise is possible between what we would like to be and experience and what existence has given us. It takes a lot of courage and clear thinking to get there.

Old age thus finds its meaning in the completion of a life, a vital stage indeed, not an afterthought or a postscript. It represents both the culmination of life and the psycho-spiritual space favorable to its final resolution. Whatever was not accomplished before, in the past, is still stored up, waiting to be realized. "Each of us has inside of us the image of what we ought to become. Until that has been realized, our happiness is not perfect," the German poet Angelus Silesius said.[5] The meaning of growing old is to perfect ourselves. Do we not spend all our lives looking for that "something" that has in turn been searching for us unceasingly throughout our existence? "What we are searching for is something that has forever been seeking us out from the deepest part of our being, in order to bring us fulfillment," writes Karlfried Dürckheim, who wonders if we are trying to experiment with our innate transcendence. "This intrinsic transcendence — to which it is important to open ourselves up, because it is the force that structures our humanity — is not something formless, a vague feeling; it is trying to take on bodily form, to find embodiment in a very precise form that will express what it actually is, through its presence, its manifestation, its appearance."[6]

A life completed is a life at peace. That is why it is so important to put our lives in order and to take stock before we leave the world's stage.

It is possible that the descent into senile dementia is linked to the fact that a person is not at peace with his or her past. According to Gérald Quitaud: "The misfortune of the dementia sufferer is that he is caught between an old unresolved task that is too big for him and a fundamental anguish about death that prevents him from forging ahead. Caught between a burdensome past and a worrying and uncertain future, he leaves the world's stage little by little, burying himself alive."[7]

It is a fact that anything left in suspense from our past, such as repressed emotions and unresolved conflicts, hinders our development. If we do not become reconciled to our past, we may find ourselves joining the ever-swelling ranks of those who end their lives with dementia.

We must disentangle the skein of our lives and wind our wool into a ball, review our past, event by event, untying all the knots one by one. The aim is to free ourselves from the shackles of a painful past and forgive ourselves for our failures. It is a work of introspection. Can we go so far as to claim that a person grows old better if he or she has had psychoanalysis or psychotherapy? I think so, insofar as this work on the self comes down to accepting reality and its inherent limits. Emotions, which are always a sign of difficulty in accepting what is, are recognized, welcomed, and worked through within the framework of these therapies, and the individual emerges from the process at peace and with a greater perspective on life.

As a therapist, I have seen how frequently human beings repress their emotions, and the pain they feel in expressing them naturally. Either they deny them or they underestimate them or they fight them. Emotions that have been locked away in a cupboard since childhood emerge — sometimes suddenly — once the vulnerability of old age opens the door to them. We then witness an outpouring of feelings held too long in check. This torrent of emotions may be uncontrollable, and the individual may collapse beneath the weight of old age. In the face of so much untimely excitement, the elderly person may develop psychosomatic problems; or his mind may slip away, as is the case in dementia; or, again, he may lapse into continual complaining, in search of impossible consolation.

When the time comes to take stock, everything that has remained in suspense, everything that was never experienced or attempted, rises up from the depths. When everything that gave meaning to life crumbles, "the Shadow" emerges in the form of bitterness, sensitivity, and whining complaints.[8] According to Karlfried Dürckheim, "In old people, many infirmities are the expression of repression, a somatization of things that have been held back for decades . . . guilty feelings, aggression, disillusionment, unshed tears, repressed anger." The realities of life block the individual's progress toward the depths of his being "in which he might find that Plenitude which is promised to him as a man."[9]

We must face up to our regrets and our remorse, the feelings of "I could have" or "I should have." As long as we do not tackle these too late, we can still draw up a balance sheet in our sixties and act on certain desires or plans that are close to our hearts.

It is important to have as few regrets as possible. We know how much remorse can gnaw away at the souls of the elderly. Long-repressed guilt rises back to the surface, causing a devaluation of the self and a loss of self-esteem. We must succeed in making peace with ourselves so that a restoration of self-esteem is possible.

My experience as a therapist has taught me that once the Shadow has been integrated — that is to say, recognized and taken into account — the individual may attain an experience of being that provides real fulfillment. Many times I have helped elderly people enter into a relationship with this "darkness." I instruct them to write down conflicts that have remained in suspense and that weigh heavily on their hearts. The ability to freely transcribe what weighs you down with guilt, fills you with anger, or makes you view the past with disenchantment — to express everything with absolute sincerity — brings a profound feeling of relief and a real liberation.

My patients did not always read to me what they had written, and I respected their privacy. To tell the truth, the mere fact of writing it all down is what liberated them. But often it was important to them that I witness what was barricading their ability to achieve personal fulfillment. The same situations recurred time and again: a father who was terrifying and inaccessible, absent, or unjust; a mother who was cold and who rejected her children, or who, on the contrary, was all-consuming, possessive, and overpresent; a sadistic brother or sister; an abusive schoolmaster — in short, situations that prevented people from being themselves and from blossoming freely. Some of these documents were addressed to people who were no longer alive, and yet they remained present and active in my patients' unconscious minds. Once liberated, these patients could then progress toward what really mattered.

## Solitude Is Golden

"Growing old is the most solitary of journeys," Benoîte Groult wrote.[10] Working at growing old implies accepting a form of solitude. I am careful to say "solitude" and not "isolation," for we now know how frequently isolation can be a source of sadness and withdrawal, which in turn can lead to an unhappy old age.

On the contrary, the kind of solitude we are discussing here is a sign of an old age that has been accepted joyfully. "Solitude is a royal gift which we push away because in that state we find ourselves infinitely free, and because freedom is the thing for which we are least prepared,"[11] wrote Jacqueline Kelen.

In her book *L'esprit de solitude* (The Spirit of Solitude), she distinguishes between the sad, painful solitude of old people who have been abandoned, forgotten, and pushed aside — which would more correctly be termed isolation — and a form of solitude that is "beautiful and courageous, rich and radiant, practiced by many sages, artists, saints, and philosophers."[12] As I read this, I wonder why we do not all have access to this magnificent solitude as we grow old. Instead of closing in upon ourselves and withdrawing, why shouldn't we set out to meet ourselves; why shouldn't we gain in perspective and continue to grow?

Look around you. So many old people are isolated because they have created a void around themselves. The cause of this void is their own acute self-centeredness, not other people's indifference. They never stop whining, complaining, and being obsessed with themselves. These "negative solitudes" lead to sadness, repetition, and despair.

Another kind of solitude is possible. At once both full and light, it brings openness and receptiveness. This solitude is ontological, for it is possible only if one has made contact with the kernel of one's own being, by which I mean "that part of me which is indestructible, sovereign, and cannot be attacked. Some call it the Spirit."[13] Let us remember the words of Sister Emmanuelle: when one is in contact with the Spirit inside oneself, one never feels isolated or cut off.

Our generation should learn how to live with itself, but we all do the complete opposite. Nobody teaches us how to be alone, and that is the case from childhood onward. The aim of all our education, whether it is dispensed by the family or school, is never to leave the child in silence, alone with himself. He is obliged to play with others, to be part of a sports team, and he is placed in front of the television. If he isolates himself, people get worried, for exploring one's inner garden is not well received. So it is hardly a surprise that the adult individual is so dependent on others, that he has never learned self-reliance, self-knowledge, or how to trust himself.

Solitude is regarded as a plague; we have a pathological view of it, so we try to avoid it at all costs. It is treated like an illness, but it is an experience that leads to freedom, to hitherto unsuspected resources and latent energies. The human individual is much more capable than we think of accepting solitude, confronting it, and living through it as an initiatory experience.

When approached in this way, the ordeal of solitude is liable to provoke an awakening, a realization. Of course, it cleanses and strips away, but it also reveals the very heart of one's being, which is made of gold: "The heart of being is joy, lightness, and freshness, but one must first unblock the spring, leave behind the showy rags, abandon the 'old man,' his sufferings and his certainties."[14]

# THE HEART
## DOES NOT GROW OLD

"When old age comes, man grows young again. That is what is happening to me now," wrote Hermann Hesse.[1]

I remember my friend Michel, a bright-eyed widower of eighty-five, a former lung specialist who was passionate about morpho-psychology. He was a charming old gentleman, and we often lunched together at the Pied de Cochon, one of his favorite brasseries. Our time together passed swiftly, for he never failed to capture my attention, and he had a gift for listening to others. Sitting opposite him, I felt inevitably spellbound by the amorous glint in his eyes, for Michel was without a doubt one of the world's lovers: a lover of life, nature, and women. He also drew remarkably well. On one occasion, when I was due to deliver a seminar on the theme of dying at a Buddhist center in the Dordogne, we were staying in the same nearby bed-and-breakfast.

One night, he produced a drawing in the silence of his room and slipped it under my door. It depicted a boat floating idly on the water, in the moonlight, and was accompanied by a poem filled with nostalgia and tact. I was touched and intrigued by this romantic gesture from such an elderly man, and at breakfast the following morning I thanked him, then added: "You're still quite a romantic!" It was then that he said to me: "It's terrible to be old in other people's eyes, when you feel as if you're still eighteen!" His heart, he said, had remained young, and he still had the emotions and urges of a young man: something that I could see in his eyes, something that had remained steady though the rest of his body had withered. Those eyes were full of mischief, joy, life, and astonishment.

This old friend then told me something that I hear from the majority of the eighty-year-olds I know. They don't feel old at all! On average, they feel ten years younger than their age and estimate that they have more time left to live than they actually have.

My friend Michel often said that he felt as if he had eternity ahead of him. In fact, he died from a pulmonary embolism shortly after the episode I have just recounted, one day during the Christmas season.

■ ■ ■ ■

Christopher, my ex-husband, is about to turn eighty. He sometimes writes poems, one of which testifies to this universal youthfulness of heart. He admits that he sometimes feels as if he were still seventeen. This is what he writes:

Of course there are things I can do no
   more,
But there are others I can and couldn't
   before.
All things, including my life have an end,
It may be to-morrow, or just round the
   bend.
In the meantime however I've more time,
   not less,
More time to love, more time to bless
All those I have known and loved in the
   past,
Love for a moment, love meant to last.
They are all of them with me, down deep
   in my heart,
They are trying to tell me that love is an
   art.[2]

And this is how he ends:

I'm lucky!

171

This is a nice way of saying that old age cannot be reduced to a series of losses and diminutions; it is a nice way of saying that old age brings new things. In the past, well-known and famous people have said such things as: "I feel that I am becoming young in my old age. I feel that a life exists beneath the old self."[3] Or: "I know very well that I am not growing old and that on the contrary I am growing; and it is this which makes me feel the approach of death. What proof of the soul's existence! My body declines, my mind grows; in my old age, there is a blossoming."[4]

Therein lies the paradox. As I have just explained, if we work at growing old, we can attain real youthfulness: emotional youthfulness, the youthfulness of the heart.

## The Richness of Time

Anyone who pays attention as they grow old will see that although one's physical vitality and certain faculties may fade, life continues to grow and expand its network of connections, and this process keeps on happening right to the end.

This feeling of still being young, experienced by so many people over eighty, testifies to a phenomenon that the philosopher Robert Misrahi has explained very clearly.

I encountered him at a seminar on old age that was organized by the Eisai Foundation. He is a small, round man whose large eyes dominate his face, and is a specialist in Spinoza. Throughout the sessions in which he participated, he maintained a dynamic view of old age, challenging us to change the way we looked at it.

Well aware that he was contradicting the current popular view, that of existential decay, Robert Misrahi lamented the fact that people today are so distressed by signs of aging and the approach of death that they give up "on the fecundity of time" and sometimes fall into such despair that they die of not dying.

"There is an unhappy awareness of growing old. . . . Strictly speaking, the subject is no longer living his life; he is living his death. In his eyes, nothing is worthwhile anymore; his life itself is worthless."[5]

He then asked if we believed that old age was still worth the trouble of living through, whether life is still meaningful in old age, and if it is worth prolonging ever further.

Robert Misrahi emphasized that magnificent expression "the fecundity of time," and insisted that, contrary to all appearances, an elderly person may continue to feel desire and be borne along by a vital impulse even when the future is hidden from view. Old age can be a process of opening up, not closing down.

This is a perspective that I have constantly supported throughout this work, a perspective that has been strengthened by the testimonies I have received. Robert Misrahi reminds us that certain individuals can experience old age "in confident serenity and tranquil patience," and that "what is possible elsewhere can be real here, what was once real can be true tomorrow."[6] I know that this view of old age must be put forward and defended.

It's all a question of desire. In his writing, Robert Misrahi challenges the pessimistic view of desire, recognized by psychoanalysis as a frantic quest doomed to failure and emptiness. "Desire is not the reign of the impossible, as is too often claimed," he declares. On the contrary, desire is a form of dynamism, which aims at joy and reciprocal relationships with others. "If the essence of man is desire," he writes, "then the pursuit of joy is his vocation."[7]

This enables us to look quite differently at growing old. The experience of growing old depends upon what is contained within the consciousness, what has been nourished by the ambient culture and by the values and beliefs each person holds. Because of its autonomy, the content of consciousness can be changed or improved. For example, an elderly person may lapse into renunciation of desire. If so, this negation of consciousness, which is a source of suffering, can be altered. It can be combated.

But at the same time, desire is always placed before "the other." There is an essential "spectator aspect," Robert Misrahi claims. It is the duty of the other to facilitate "the transition from the negative to the positive" through the way he views the elderly person, who is seeking reciprocity and recognition.

Robert Misrahi calls upon others to take up this responsibility. He appeals to medicine, and especially gerontology, whose task it is to "work toward the best possible preservation of life forces, since the joy of living is the highest good."[8]

But while medicine can restore physical vitality, it cannot, on its own, change awareness. Isn't it up to society as a whole to change the way it looks at old age, to shoulder this responsibility? If so, this means that it is up to each one of us, as it is an issue that concerns us all.

Robert Misrahi calls for a "spiritual conversion" — such a complete transformation in the awareness of growing old that it could truly be called a new beginning. He argues that we can be reborn to life when we are very old — even if our physical universe has shrunk, even if the pace of life has slowed down.

"Instead of regarding his old age as a form of decline, isolation, and an ending, the subject may now perceive in himself the serene, fertile movement of new life. After effective treatment and above all after a sort of 'psychological' and philosophical reeducation, the elderly subject can enter a new period of existence that, with the presence and active warmth of loved ones and friends, can amount to an awakening and to the emergence of a new impetus and a new desire to live."[9]

I have heard Robert Misrahi deliver a powerful defense of this idea that we should teach the old to grow old, to reeducate them so that they see old age as a chance for a veritable rebirth. He envisages this reeducation as taking place on three levels: creativity, joy, and serenity in the face of death.

All of this can be taught. And Robert Misrahi believes that rather than invest so much energy in activities and pretend celebrations that aim only to "fill in the boredom of empty, passive time," it would be better to invite the elderly subjects to travel mentally, to think through their lives, listen to music, read, write, contemplate, explore works of art, walk, or meditate. In short, they should be invited to live! Some psychologists do this in retirement homes, flushing out life from the corners where it huddles but still exists. "With very elderly people, we have no other choice but to act as fishers of life, using our landing nets to catch small joys. An important part of our work consists perhaps in surprising people with things they no longer dared hope for," one of them wrote.[10]

Can we learn at sixty, seventy, or eighty to liberate our buried creativity if we have not done so earlier in life? Yes! It is never too late to set out to meet ourselves, and to liberate the feelings or emotions we have been holding prisoner. It is never too late to develop our creativity, rediscover our childhood souls, and trust our intuition. Referring to her husband's old age, Maud Mannoni wrote: "Old age is a state of mind. There are old twenty-year-olds and young eighty-year-olds. It is a matter of being generous of heart, and staying true to the child one used to be."[11]

## Activities and Actions

I admire the way some activity leaders help the elderly to rediscover their childhood souls. For example, Yves Penay, a man of the theater and a director, has for several years been running theater workshops for elderly people. Around a dozen people aged between sixty and eighty, most of them women, attend his sessions every week. At the start, their motivation is essentially to exercise their memory, but very quickly everyone realizes that something much more important is at stake. Using scenes from his theatrical repertoire, Yves offers them a chance to explore the multiple facets of their personalities as honestly as possible. It is exciting work. The people he sees arriving are rather inhibited, but as the sessions progress they discover resources they never knew they had. One, a former executive secretary, takes unexpected pleasure in playing the part of a queen; another, a sensible wife and mother, discovers the depths of passion. Yves sees his students positively blossoming, opening up to the whole spectrum of their emotions. There's nothing like it for keeping a person alive.

When he began this experiment, Yves found that these individuals living in their third and fourth age were as fresh and receptive as his adolescent pupils. "They are incredibly physically fit, and as they no longer have job or family responsibilities and have all the time they want, you'd swear they have their whole lives ahead of them!" he explained to me.

"Do they work hard?" I asked.

"Yes. I suggest that they put on a performance every six months, to which they can invite their friends, so they come to the workshop even when they are ill; and I remember one person who came on crutches after a bad fall.

"I often remind them of Sarah Bernhardt saying 'Nevertheless!' And that spurs them on. Indeed, Sarah Bernhardt acted until she was seventy-five, and everyone knows that her interpretation of *L'Aiglon* was a triumph. Age loses its importance when you act with heart and passion."

**Living in the Now**

Next, suggests Robert Misrahi, we must teach a new kind of wisdom: not stoic resignation but a new way of looking at the life that is coming to an end. "Human life is not condemned to suffering," he says, but destined for joy, happiness, and serenity. The present must be lived for itself, a rich, fulfilled now. In order to rejoice in the present moment, the elderly subject must "rediscover his ability to be enchanted and amazed." He says that "if converted to life, old age can successfully turn the present moment into a delight" by opening the individual up to enchantment.[12]

I have given a great deal of thought to what Spinoza said: "Delight in the present moment constantly enriches time."[13] All life's joys and works continue, while other joys also come along, setting our hearts aquiver and making us feel that we are fully alive. Famously, the philosopher stated: "We are experiencing being eternal."[14] We should understand this to refer to the unprecedented experience of an eternity that is not an afterlife in terms of time but a form of inner fulfillment.

As we grow older, we should rejoice that we are still alive, and not lament the fact that we are approaching death: this is the wise advice that Robert Misrahi gives us. We should take inspiration from the radiant old people we know as we attempt to cultivate our ability to experience joy, wonderment, and gratitude. We should stop paying attention to the changes in our body and our physical image, and allow the part of ourselves that does not grow old to live. "This is the final gift of a person who reaches old age: passing on 'a message of joyful maturity' to those who are still alive, and who, when they, too, are old, will surely remember that there is a way of growing old that does not burden loved ones but, on the contrary, helps them to live."[15]

Robert Misrahi is explicit in what we should pass on to younger generations: the image of a generation that is happy to grow old and to find completion. Implementing this "rebirth" as we enter the third or fourth age is a bold undertaking, and it will succeed only if we maintain our connections with others, if we both give and receive love. It is clear that the success of our efforts will depend to a large extent upon affection, benevolence, and human warmth that is sincere rather than conventional.

Robert Misrahi's hoped-for education in living a happy old age has already been implemented in some places: for example, the philosopher Bertrand Vergely is increasingly in demand among pensioners' cultural circles, whose participants have the time to devote to philosophical reflection. When I went to hear him speak during one of his "Philosophy Tuesdays," he delivered a superb lecture on the meaning of life.[16] I was not surprised to see that around 80 percent of the audience were senior citizens, and the majority of them were women. The auditorium was full to bursting, and the attentive faces in the audience displayed real pleasure, almost jubilation. This large audience and the success of the lecture suggest that there may be a newfound desire in our society — certainly in France — to think about one's life. As Gilles Deleuze noted: "When old age comes, bringing with it the time to speak in precise terms, there is one question we ask in discreet agitation, at midnight, when we have nothing left to ask: 'What was my life all about?' We've asked it before; in fact, we've never stopped asking it, but it was too indirect or oblique, too artificial, or too abstract, and we merely aired it, mentioning it in passing rather than being consumed by it."[17]

Finally, the last commitment that Robert Misrahi hopes will be taken up by people who are growing old is educating others about a new relationship with death. Death does not necessarily mean expiring tragically, but as long as it continues to be perceived as a catastrophe, as ending a life that should last forever, it will appear absurd and scandalous. "A death devoid of reason would retroactively remove all possible meaning from life, because it would forever nullify and cancel out any action whatsoever."[18] So we must turn the way we look at death upside down. Instead of regarding our own end as the primordial element of our existence, it must be considered as an inevitable but secondary element. "The important thing," according to Robert Misrahi, is to "reendow the living present with all its intensity and all its richness."[19]

# A Sensual Old Age

"The acceptance of a new sexuality," writes Robert Misrahi, "may eventually contribute to an improvement of old age."[1]

The sexuality of elderly people is one of our society's last taboos. Without question, more is said about men's sexuality — for example, when we talk about some old men's lubricious desires, or the drama of male impotence. Not a word is spoken about the sexuality of old women, as if they no longer feel desire or are no longer desirable after menopause. As we shall see in the pages that follow, this is not the case.

The European TV channel Arte recently devoted a themed evening to the sexuality of old people.[2] The men and women featured in this documentary spoke of their desires and their fears, their relationship with their own bodies, and their new approach to eroticism. Some spoke with modesty and tenderness; others, with humor.

One woman complained that she no longer met anyone: "I can't understand why. People say to me: You're still beautiful. The truth is that I meet nobody, nobody. I don't know if it's because people are becoming more demanding. In any event, when a man smiles at me, I feel alive. For me, it's eroticism. . . . I think it's inhuman, the rule that says that a person is no longer worthy of being looked at after a certain age, or when she has a certain number of wrinkles. It's really terrible!"

What she said was confirmed by the psychotherapist Ulrike Brandenburg, who regarded the sex lives of elderly women as very sad: "I hear women aged around sixty or seventy saying to me: I no longer exist, I'm not on the scene anymore when it comes to sex. Nobody notices me anymore! Men can have erections, thanks to new products that enhance virility, so why can't we see women as radiant, gray-haired, and sensual?"

Over recent months, I have looked at women of my own age and older with new eyes. Often, I have considered them beautiful. Admittedly, their bodies have aged, but they have an emotional beauty that makes them fortunate enough to retain their desires — and that is perhaps the key.

One of the advantages of maturity is that people are freer and more receptive. There is a factual freedom, as the children have grown up and left the family nest, and work considerations are a thing of the past. There is also an inner freedom, because maturity means no longer clinging to youth, and accepting growing old. These mature individuals live their remaining time in the present moment.

Women of my age see things clearly; they know that they are not eternal, and that this is one more reason for dwelling in the present, aware of their bodies, in charge of their desires. I find them more sensual than ever. They savor life without haste or anxiety, and that is what constitutes their charm and makes them desirable.

Someone recently told me about an encounter between a seventy-three-year-old woman writer who is almost blind and a man twenty years younger. This woman has a passion for music, and the encounter took place during an organized group trip, no doubt linked to this theme. As she cannot see very well, this man helped her several times: crossing the street, or going up and down stairs. She instantly loved his gentle, attentive hands. And she said to herself: "If his penis is like his hands, well . . . !" As she is a woman of infinite charm, it's easy to imagine what happened next.

What are the mechanisms of an elderly man or woman's sexual attraction? I am aware that I am tackling a question that nobody dares discuss. We are so fixated on youthful norms that we find it difficult to imagine the amorous interplay between an old body and one that is still young, and even harder to imagine two bodies withered by age. What is this desire, which is fed not by form or aesthetic beauty but by something else? It is stimulated by the pleasure of being together in a joining of hearts, by the softness of skin, by the pace and presence of the other person, and by the emotion of the encounter.

It is time to wring the neck of the aesthetic decree that demands that aging women transform their faces into expressionless masks in order to make themselves young and remain desirable. I do not think that a sixty-five-year-old woman's "lifted" face can express a flicker of emotion. True, the wrinkles are softened, and the skin is stretched like the skin of a drum, but the face is no longer expressive. The marks of time, and all traces of the joys and sorrows that have come her way, have been erased. Who can honestly say that a lifted face is beautiful? Our true definition of beauty relies on something else, and this "something else" is intimately tied to emotion. It is what we call charm: the depth of a look, an expression in the eyes, a dazzling smile. Charm does not grow old, nor does emotion. In fact, both can even gain in depth and intensity with age.

It is time to convince women to love their aging faces, to train their inner spotlight on the expression in their eyes and their smiles rather than on their crow's-feet, the bags under their eyes, or their drooping eyelids. It is time to help them bring their faces back to life, and to recognize that this life, this radiance, is the very essence of their beauty.

This presupposes that women stop looking at themselves in the mirror and direct their energy toward experiences that make the soul quiver: gazing at the beauty of a setting sun or a starry sky, marveling at an affectionate gesture between two people who love each other, being intoxicated by a jazz concert or a Bach chorale.

It is a particular kind of eros that unites the elderly man and woman. Nancy Huston's expression "melting joy" comes to mind.[3] Without question, the mature or elderly woman gives herself more deeply; she opens up her body and her being more fully. "I felt as if I were swimming in her, like in an ocean," says one of my Greek friends, aged sixty-five, in an attempt to translate the delicious feeling of well-being and inner vastness he experienced when he made love to a woman older than he was.

"A woman's aging body is not a frightening image for me," testifies another guest on Arte. "It doesn't take away my desire to make love to her. It's the general appearance that counts, the harmony that radiates from her. It doesn't matter if she has small breasts or pendulous breasts! Similarly, her skin may be lined, but I don't care about that if I like her eyes. There you are, that's how I see things. With increasing age, sexuality is more beautiful, it lasts longer, and it is more erotic. You're slower, and you share more affectionate gestures and caresses. At the end of the day, I think pleasure is more intense and more satisfying."[4]

Why are we so oversensitive when it comes to talking about elderly people's sexuality? Doubtless it is not "erotically correct" to talk about a quasi-spiritual experience, an experience of completeness and communion that far exceeds the pleasure of orgasm.

"When I talk about spirituality in the loving relationship, it is for example when he and I are together, in a state close to meditation, motionless, as if we are linked to the universe. It is an absolute pleasure but without a climax, without an orgasm; the happiness of being. It is like meeting God himself. . . . Everything in us opens up to the other person and to the world. It's a state of abandon."[5]

It seems obvious that when we grow old, we fall in love not with the other person's physique but with his or her presence.

Of course, there are women who never recover from a collapse in self-esteem. When they no longer consider themselves fit to be seen or desirable, they bury their own sensuality and desire. They do not want to "inflict" the sight of their misshapen bodies on a man. Quite simply, they can no longer bear themselves, and that is that. They will never make love again. This renunciation of desire leads more quickly than one might imagine to real old age, to an absence of joy and vitality, and to a dried-up heart.

In the eighteenth century, someone asked the Princess Palatine at what age sexual desire disappeared. She replied: "How should I know? I'm only eighty!"

Today, however, many people believe that the elderly no longer have any desires, or sexual life. People think that even if they wanted to, they could not make love; and if they did make love, it would be something shameful, even perverted.

Twenty-eight years ago, an American study involving about two hundred people aged between 80 and 102 showed that 63 percent of the men and 30 percent of the women still had sex; 72 percent of the men and 40 percent of the women masturbated; and 82 percent of the men and 64 percent of the women had affectionate relationships.[6]

Deirdre Fishel's film *Still Doing It: The Intimate Lives of Women Over 65* is a portrait of several American women aged between sixty-five and eighty-seven who were not afraid to demand their right to an active sexual life.[7]

Those who think that elderly women have given up all forms of sexuality are in for a shock. In this documentary, it is made clear that menopause does not signal the end of sexual life — quite the reverse. Women are liberated by the fact that they are now free from contraception and have finished raising their children. Many women begin intense loving relationships after the age of sixty-five. "I discovered after menopause that the desire was still there," states one of the women. "I told myself that I was too old to make love, but then I told myself that if my body wanted to, it was because it was still young enough to do it."

At the age of eighty-five, Frances has the good fortune to be involved in a very intense relationship with a lover younger than her, the journalist David Sternberg, whom she'd met five years earlier. "David is the great love of my life," she says. Although she was obliged to go into a retirement home after breaking her hip, the relationship continued. This elderly woman is aware that the majority of people see her only as an old woman in her wheelchair, but she still continues to make love: "When I make love, no one else matters. I am in my world, David is in his, and nothing else is important. In a retirement home we don't have much privacy, but we do what we can. We're happy with what we can offer each other."

The sexologist Betty Dodson, aged seventy-three, is also in a happy relationship, with her twenty-six-year-old lover, Eric, who has been living with her for the past four years. Eric admits that Betty no longer has the body of a young girl, but he wouldn't give up his relationship with this "astonishing woman" for anything. He adores her experience and her ability to express her desire: "It surprised me that she was so seductive at sixty-nine. I remember the first time she undressed. Obviously she no longer had a young woman's body. That made me feel a little uneasy, but I told myself that I had a lot to gain by setting aside these petty-minded considerations of appearance," the young man confides. And Betty adds: "I asked myself the same questions. I said to myself, My God, I'm going to have to get undressed, and with my aging body, I'm going to be face-to-face with a superb young body. I had to do it in a rush." Eric recognizes that if Betty had been unhappy with her body image, it would have damaged their relationship. Betty confirms that all women have to take up this challenge, and she is constantly fighting for them not to throw in the towel. "If we have to live in a world where you can't have sexual relations unless you're beautiful and young, that's distressing! I have never been so much in harmony with a man in all my life. And yet many people find it repugnant that I have such a young lover!"

Ellen and Dolores met three years ago: Ellen is sixty-eight; Dolores, seventy. Ellen ended a long, unsatisfactory heterosexual union in order to live with Dolores, and together they are working to set up retirement homes for gays and lesbians. "When people stand up on the bus to give us their seats, they have absolutely no idea how wild we are in bed!" Ellen exclaims.

As for Ruth, who remarried at sixty-nine, this period of her life has been a time of renewal. Ruth's husband admits: "The first time we made love, age didn't matter at all. It was like being in love for the first time."

Elaine is a grandmother and great-grandmother, and yet she has had a lover for twenty years. "Physical intimacy with someone brings its own element. My life is complete. This little piece of the puzzle makes all the difference."

Only Freddie, a widow for twenty years, remarks that there are few free men her age. She has given up entirely on having a sexual life. "After Sydney's death, I suppressed all my sexual desires, and tried not to think about them anymore. But sometimes they emerged unexpectedly, intensely, and I was surprised that these sensations were still so strong. I looked around me to see if there were any available men, but I thought I would have to make the first move, and personally I am not very good at doing that. It was as if nobody was looking at me. The men seemed to be looking for younger women." Freddie talks about this buried sexual life as if it were a dream. She remembers that she used to make love and that it was good. Now she refuses to feel sorry for herself.

Finally there is Harriet, a former model: "For me, making love is a moment of pure happiness. Even when it doesn't work out, it's better than doing without." We see her in discussion with women of her age. The majority agree that they still have sexual needs but that they have renounced all sexuality. Harriet, on the other hand, has not: "Life has always been full of surprises for me. Someone has always popped up at the right moment. My mother — God rest her soul — used to say: 'Men are like trams; you miss one, and then the next one turns up a few minutes later.' The only thing is that now they take a bit longer to arrive!"

Contrary to certain popular ideas, sexuality does not disappear with age. This myth does, however, contain a few truths. Although desire, pleasure, and orgasm are all possible throughout one's life, elderly people are in fact more limited in their love-making. They have sexual relations less often and find it more difficult to attain orgasm. Anatomical and physiological changes — including loss of moisture and elasticity in the vagina after menopause, and the absence of an erection — often bring about a halt in sexual activity.

We do not really know what goes on in the privacy of the bedroom, and these generalizations probably conceal a wide variety of situations. Some individuals may be satisfied to liberate themselves completely from sexuality, while others remain full of desire and continue to be sexually active. Olivier de Ladoucette cites the example of one couple of octogenarians "who thought that the page had turned. Then they took a trip to Venice and experienced the awakening of sensations they no longer even thought about."[8]

Any sex life in later years is a continuation of whatever it was earlier in a person's life. Individuals who are fulfilled by an imaginative, rich, and harmonious sex life will remain sexually active as they grow older, although perhaps to a lesser degree. On the other hand, some people have little or no interest in "it," and it would be surprising if this attitude changed as they grew older.

Age, therefore, does not dictate sexual desire, even though it may alter its frequency and characteristics. While sexual relations may be slower and less active, we know that they also become more sensual.

"When I was younger, desire was more

frequent. But now the orgasms are slower and more intense," declares one of the women in Deirdre Fishel's film. "I feel freer, more inventive. When I was younger, I believed that I had to make a lot of noise to show my partner that we were exceptional lovers. Now I believe that is a burden. Because I am more at ease with myself, I am more at ease in my sexuality. I think that at our age we must accept the fact that we have changed, and move on to other things, paying more attention to caresses. There are so many ways of experiencing pleasure. For me, the caresses are more important than the act itself. It's important to pay attention to the other person, to the preliminaries. The men I have known think that it's not worth the bother of making love now that they're not 'performers' anymore. I think they are wrong. Sexual relations are a way of expressing one's love. That is why we miss them so much. We need to be taken in someone's arms, to be touched."

There is a whole range of sensations and sensual contacts to be discovered: the feeling of being close to each other, sleeping skin against skin, cuddling.

During a cruise we were taking in Sardinia, Jean-François Deniau, who was then almost seventy-five, told me that despite his heart problems he frequently made love, but "in a lazy way." That was his way of praising gentle sensual pleasure.

Alain Moreau writes that people make love better at sixty than at twenty. We must not, he says, confuse desire with the erection, for they are two very different things: "There is no reason to underplay the roles of sensation and imagination; on the contrary, they are strengthened by the loss of inhibitions, and therefore their scope and their efficacy are increased. Because of the additional control it permits, the weakening of blood pressure and raw sex drive offers many more possibilities for pleasures, joys, and happiness than it takes away."[9]

The couples aged over seventy-two whom I have spoken to who still make love all told me that the woman's attitude was fundamental in their pursuit of sexual activity. It is obvious that if a woman loses confidence in herself following menopause and feels that she is responsible for her partner's failure to perform, she will become mired in the belief that she is less attractive and, consequently, sound the death knell of their sex life. If, on the other hand, she retains confidence in herself, and does not feel wounded or frustrated by her companion's temporary — or even permanent — impotence, they will make light of it and look for another way of making love.

Sexuality increases longevity. Although little has been written about the contribution of a flourishing sexual life to growing old happily, one can imagine how much it could contribute in terms of psychological equilibrium and self-esteem.[10]

Yet the taboo remains. Although today we are slightly more accepting of the fact that elderly men and women are drawn together in their loneliness, and that they may show each other friendship and affection, we are much less receptive to the idea that they might indulge in the act of sex. In the eyes of the young, but also in the eyes of older people who were brought up to believe in the sins of the flesh, old people's sexuality remains scandalous, even disgusting. In *The Night of the Shooting Stars,* a film by the Taviani brothers, an old man and an old woman find themselves sleeping in the same bedroom, and they make love. "The talent of these two filmmakers was necessary to make this scene beautiful and acceptable, for the images of such happy sexuality are still provocative," writes Jean-Louis Servan-Schreiber.[11] Even today, the image of an old couple doing anything other than sitting platonically on a bench gazing at the sea generates a feeling of unease. Sex between senior citizens seems "incompatible with the aesthetic canons of politically correct eroticism."[12]

This shameful view of old people's sexuality is now being questioned by the baby boomers. People of this generation have known contraception and sexual freedom, and were the pioneers of a moral revolution. They contributed to the separation of pleasure and procreation, and helped to remove the guilt from extramarital love. They are not ready to give up on physical love as they get older, and scientific progress is helping them.

In spite of this, elderly people's sexuality will continue to remain taboo for a long time, perhaps even forever, for reasons that are not cultural but more profound, even subconscious. Just as children cannot imagine their parents making love, we as adults cannot visualize older people being sexually active, and this is undoubtedly why their sexuality is so frowned upon in retirement homes.

"A few years ago," recalls Paulette Guinchard, "the director of a unit whose staff I was training insisted that I talk about sexuality. There, I discovered that carers often find themselves alone, dealing with behavior that they do not understand, and which they reject as ugly, dirty, and incongruous. They may condemn it with very harsh words; and some may even go so far as to ask doctors for treatments to calm down the 'guilty' parties."[13] Paulette Guinchard was aware of carers' reservations and even violent reactions to the sexuality that the elderly residents exhibited. Certain carers expressed brutal judgments — for example, by demanding that an old woman's masturbation "should be punished or at least treated," or declaring that "only old pigs would display so provocatively that they have this kind of need, desire, or pleasure."

Increasingly, this question is being covered in training programs for staff who work in retirement homes. Once carers are aware that this dimension is still active in the residents' private lives, they are capable of respecting it. At the same time, magazines aimed at the third age are also beginning to devote special reports to the topic.

"How long will it be before we see double beds in retirement homes?" wonders Paulette Guinchard. "At the moment, single beds are almost universally the only available option, clearly demonstrating that sexuality is not an established phenomenon, and that it is in fact officially denied, even prohibited. . . . The old have their own ideas on the subject, but nobody asks them. Take this old lady, for instance: 'I hope that if I have to go into a retirement home, I will have a double bed and that I won't be made to sleep in a single bed like when I was at boarding school. That would make me feel that I was no longer an individual who could welcome another person into her bed!' "[14]

In France, the Elderly Person's Charter of 1995 guarantees the right to a private life in one's own room. Thus, officially, every individual is free to love at any age, while of course respecting the usual proprieties.

A middle ground must be found between the two extremes: on the one hand, overtly displaying one's sexuality in an attempt to gain attention and turning it into the subject of a political battle; and on the other, denying and denigrating it, as is too often the case. The key is to respect people's private lives.

It is difficult to find the right tone in which to talk about old people's sexuality. Without question, the only way to do so is by showing that it is different: internalized, infinitely more affectionate, slower, and more sensual. It is an emotional kind of sexuality, guided not by the sex drive but by the heart. Never in the life of a human being is the expression "making love" more meaningful than when it refers to a loving, knowing encounter between bodies that are aging or already old.

## Harold and Élise

I would not want to end this chapter on sexuality in old age without including the words of eighty-year-old Harold, who still frequently makes love to seventy-year-old Élise. They both agreed to talk to me.

Harold is a Taoist. For twenty years he has been practicing the Tao of love, a Chinese spiritual path that instructs its followers to lead a healthy life, with the full enjoyment of both earthly and celestial pleasures. Love and sexuality are among these pleasures, and are in fact their source. Without the harmony of yin and yang, everything ends in destruction and death, and all destruction, hatred, and greed are born out of a desperate lack of love and sexual contact. This goes to show how important sexual contact is to good health, well-being, and longevity.

Longevity is an obsession among the Chinese. As long as they manage to remain in good health, they regard old age as the happiest time of their lives — and a continuing sex life contributes to maintaining good health. All the writings of ancient China regard the Taoist art of love as an essential part of long life.

Harold talked to me about this revolutionary kind of sexuality, which is so very different from our Western practices, and which has never been tainted by guilt or repression.

Tao contains a number of central principles: *coitus reservatus,* or controlled ejaculation; the importance of the female orgasm; and the understanding of the fact that the male orgasm and ejaculation are not one and the same thing. Today, these principles are being widely adopted by Western sexologists, who use this art of loving to help their patients blossom.

Harold therefore practices *coitus reservatus.* Why, and how? I wanted to know more. Harold explained to me that doctors in ancient China advised men over fifty to make every effort to control their ejaculation, advising them of the dangers of ejaculating as a matter of course. "After ejaculation," Harold explained, quoting Jolan Chang's *The Tao of Love and Sex,* "the man is tired, his ears buzz, his eyes are heavy, and he wants to sleep. He is thirsty, and his limbs are unresponsive and stiff. During ejaculation, he experiences a brief moment of joy, but it leads to long hours of lassitude. This is not really sensual pleasure."[15]

The prescription for some men is to ejaculate only two or three times out of ten, while for others the figure is once in one hundred. In the words of the sixth-century Chinese doctor Soen Sse-Mo, who died at the age of 101: "If you can make love a hundred times without emission, you will live a long time."[16]

Harold told me that the older a man gets, the less he needs to ejaculate each time he makes love. Dissociating ejaculation from the sexual act brings greater freedom. When I asked him what pleasure this gave him, Harold answered that on no account would he exchange the intense pleasure he experienced now for the type of pleasure he experienced when he was younger, before he discovered the Tao. I believed him, for I could see that he was happy and at peace, and I could see that he truly enjoyed making love — there was no doubt about that. He told me that the pleasure he felt was not a kind of violent explosion but a delicious relaxation; a kind of pleasure that translated into a feeling of a release, a communion that was voluptuous and sensual and carried on into something bigger than oneself. "That is what it is," he insisted. "It is a feeling of close communion and sharing — not an individual, solitary spasm that excludes my wife." The Tao of love is a sensual practice. First, the couple must learn to breathe long and deeply in order to be relaxed; then they must open themselves up, sharpen their senses, and move their attention away from ejaculation.

What Harold described to me put me in mind of Freud's pregenitality, for this involved returning to a polymorphism that was wise, not perverse. Although Taoists stress the importance of lovemaking technique, it is the search for reciprocal harmony and serenity that is all-important. The sexual act is not purely mechanical but is a total experience. Sensory development is nourished by this harmonious sexuality: the senses of smell and touch; prolonged bodily contact; gentle, slow caresses; and affectionately spoken words.

Élise, who had remained silent up to this point, now joined in our conversation. She met Harold at the age of fifty-two; he initiated her into the Tao, though at that time she had no idea that the sexual act could bring such profound joy. She told me that it was difficult to put this ineffable experience into words. As I listened to her, I discovered an aspect of old people's sexuality I knew nothing about: they have time and a free spirit, and can appreciate and savor the touch of someone else's skin, the fact of being inside each other, the way their energies and breaths mingle. Through lovemaking, they attain an inner peace they have never known before; and there is no doubt at all that loving bodily contact and tender communion contributed to this elderly couple's well-being and harmony.

I wondered, was it tiring to have frequent sexual contact? "No," Harold replied, "quite the reverse!" For this is a relaxed kind of sexuality. The Chinese doctor Soen believed that once the two partners had attained a high level of consciousness, "they became profoundly united while remaining motionless so as not to disturb the *king* (the semen). They can practice this kind of union dozens of times in a twenty-four-hour period, and in so doing they will experience longevity."[17]

Everything Harold told me intrigued me greatly. All around me I hear men over seventy complaining about impotence and the unhappiness it causes them, and I think back to the passage from Simone de Beauvoir's *The Coming of Age* that mentions Paul Léautaud's experiences. At the age of fifty, the writer meets a woman of fifty-five who is passionate and "wondrously set up for pleasure." Seven years later, he is exhausted and reduces the frequency of sexual relations but begins to masturbate. According to the Tao of love, such behavior is nonsensical. "Those who know the Tao will understand instantly that this was not the solution. In men, masturbation leads to a loss of the masculine essence, which is not compensated for by any gain in feminine essence. Because this act lacks the harmony of yin and yang, it has no purpose."[18] The Tao has no word to designate impotence. The people of ancient China did not see it as an important problem, for the absence of an erection does not prevent an elderly man from establishing the communion of yin and yang. There are many ways of giving and receiving pleasure, a fact that Paul Léautaud failed to discover. He spent his old age in "an abyss of sadness."

If men read the Tao of love as they grew older, Harold went on, they would discover that a man can penetrate his partner without being in a state of erection, and that it is a good thing for him to abstain from ejaculating. This Chinese art of love develops the technique of nonrigid penetration, which "works a kind of miracle: close contact between a penis and a vagina without an initial erection."[19] It is this technique that Harold uses, enabling him to make love at the age of eighty. What did Élise think of it? She laughed and assured me that this type of penetration has its charms. And she reminded me of something that all sexologists know, which they should reiterate more often to correct misleading advertisements: a woman's sexual satisfaction has little to do with the size of the man's penis. "If the man matches this communion with his love and with his respect for the woman, and if he truly cares about what he is doing, how will a small difference in size or shape change things? A firm, hard member that is thrust roughly in and out is of less value than a weak, soft member that moves gently and delicately," declared Sou-Nu, the governess of Emperor Huang-Ti.[20]

Harold is convinced that practicing the Tao helps him to grow old in a positive way. As Anaïs Nin put it: "Isn't love the only magic spell against death, old age, and a humdrum existence?"[21]

# THE FECUNDITY OF TIME

"The task of being old is as beautiful and sacred as that of being young," wrote Hermann Hesse.[1]

Everyone knows that old age brings its share of aches and pains, and that death awaits us at the end of the race. Year after year we must make sacrifices and accept that there are things we have to give up. We must learn not to rely upon our senses and our strength. There are infirmities and illnesses, the failing of senses and organs, and the numerous pains we feel most acutely during nights that are often long and anguished. All of this Hermann Hesse admits as bitter reality. However, he reminds us that it would be pitiful and sad to abandon ourselves exclusively to this process of wasting away, and fail to see that old age also has its good side, its advantages, its sources of consolation and joy. "When two old people meet, they should not simply talk about their accursed gout, their stiffening limbs, and how they become out of breath when they climb steps. They should not just tell each other about their pains and their annoyances, but also relate the events and experiences that have delighted and comforted them, and they are many.

"We who have white hair derive strength, patience, and joy from sources the young know nothing about. Watching, observing, and contemplating gradually become habits and exercises, and imperceptibly all our behavior begins to be influenced by this state of mind and the attitude to which it leads."[2]

Toward the end of her life, the psychoanalyst Lou Andreas-Salomé wrote: "The closer I get to the end of my existence, the easier it becomes for me to embrace this strange thing that is life in its entirety."[3]

Let us imagine that we have said goodbye to our youth, that we are at peace with our past, that we trust in the "fecundity of time," and that we have accepted a form of solitude. Our hearts are still young, and we have found new ways of making love. This entire path has led us toward a kind of completion; we feel lighter, and have a desire to rise higher.

"At a given point in our lives, we must

jump into the void, with the desire to ascend as our only parachute," writes Lorette Nobécourt.[4]

In an interview given almost twenty years ago as he was entering the third age, Michel Serres, a great French philosopher, said that in his experience advancing age was a detachment from everything that weighed heavily upon him: the burdens of tradition, of learned truths, of family, of groups, and of society. "Growing old is the opposite of what we might think; it is rejecting preconceived ideas, and becoming lighter."[5]

Two summers ago, Alberte, an old woman from the île d'Yeu, left us all stunned when she decided to make a parachute jump during the flying club's festival. Accompanied by a young instructor, she boarded a small plane, and once they were above the island, they leaped together into the void. As their parachutes opened, she experienced one of the strongest, most beautiful emotions of her life. A few weeks later, I dined at her home, and we talked about her exploit and also about the way she lives life at her age. I found the words of this seventy-six-year-old woman full of a very simple wisdom, which was light and joyful. She is at peace with her life; she stays active by walking and singing, and has no fear of death. Like all those who have accepted growing old but who remain young in spirit, she has just one desire: to lighten her burden and see the world with different eyes.

## Consciousness Raising

The poet Chestov wrote of an angel whose wings are studded with eyes that hold the power to see beyond the superficial and the apparent. This angel approaches those who are coming to the end of their lives. What better way to describe the faculty granted to those who have accepted growing old? "There is no longer any point in languishing, sniveling, or feeling that we're the victims of a conspiracy: we must ascend, rise up toward a higher level of consciousness," writes Gérald Quitaud.[6] The symbolic task of growing old is to cast off the mooring ropes so that the hot-air balloon can rise up toward the light and leave the world of suffering. What meaning can my life have today if I refuse to be content with what is visible, if I refuse to be content with feeling sorry for myself? Can I experience fulfillment? Can I raise my level of consciousness and "create bridges between the most peripheral reality of my existence and the warm, deep, mysterious part of my being"?[7]

At his eightieth birthday celebration, the Oriental scholar Arnaud Desjardins confided to me that the key to this ascent was to let go, to accept what is. It is a difficult path, an exercise in humility, but one in which more people succeed than one might think, for eventually it leads to a feeling of lightness and joy.

Karlfried Dürckheim had the following message for anyone who was struggling with growing old: "You can let go now, let go of what was until now the center of your life. Leave it behind and start listening to what is inside you. Let go of what has concerned you as an existential being and allow your essential being to manifest itself. Begin to make your way toward maturity."[8]

In order to achieve this, we can neither resist growing old nor cling to the past, retaining or reproducing it. "One must be capable of metamorphosing, of experiencing newness by putting all one's strength into it. The feeling of sadness that comes from attachment to what has been lost is negative and does not correspond to the true meaning of life," Hermann Hesse declared.[9] Life always moves toward something new. This is the very logic of life, a logic that we all experience through the losses that punctuate our lives. Admittedly, old age obliges us to say good-bye to certain things that I have already discussed; admittedly, we see our life force and some of our faculties fade — but, on the other hand, we begin to perceive infinity.

## Meditative Action

A few years ago, I had the good fortune to take part in a "conscious walk" led by Thich Nhat Hanh, a Vietnamese Buddhist monk who founded the Village of the Plum Trees in the Dordogne, where he teaches meditation, Tai Chi, and the practice of conscious presence. It is said that this monk was once invited to New York for an international meeting on peace, where he strongly impressed the participants by walking in extremely slowly and smiling, visibly in a meditative state. He seemed to turn each step into a conscious act, and the assembled audience felt a wave of peace pass through them. He did not need to add much, for this was the message he wished to deliver: "You seek a more peaceful world. Start by establishing that peace deep inside yourselves!"

Around one hundred of us had come to experience meditative walking. Thich Nhat Hanh explained in simple terms the experiment he wanted us to carry out. First, we should quite simply observe the position of our bodies in space, feel our feet making contact with the ground, and prolong that contact, as if we had roots under the soles of our feet. Then we should perceive the space above our heads, as if an invisible antenna linked us to the sky. Next, we were to begin walking, consciously following the pace of our own breathing, with, he said, an "inner smile." We should walk slowly, conscious of the happiness of being alive, and whisper inwardly: "I breathe in, I breathe out, deeper, more softly."

"Little by little," he said, "you will experience a feeling of calm, freedom, and joy entering you; you will feel firmly rooted on your base."

It was true, and since then, each time I walk I think of that experience and practice meditative walking. I seriously think that it should be taught to senior citizens — to those who want to remain as men and women on the move and those who fear immobility and the brittleness of old age.

Even when we have aged somewhat, walking is not just for the lucky few. Progress in orthopedic surgery has enabled seventy- and eighty-year-olds to frisk about with brand-new hips! And even if we no longer have the tendons and the heart of a twenty-year-old, walking, swimming, and cycling remain sports that we can go on practicing, for we can do these activities at our own pace. All one has to do is spend a week in the mountains to realize that the paths are filled with people in their third or fourth age.

During a recent trip to the Valais, in Switzerland, I was sitting on a bench admiring the sweeping view down to the Val d'Anniviers when an old man emerged from a path and came to sit down beside me, to catch his breath. When I expressed surprise that he had climbed so high at his age — we were eighteen hundred meters up — he told me this: "I walk for an hour every day; it's my daily sport. I train because, you see, each summer I treat myself and walk up as far as the Weisshorn Hotel." He pointed to a large white building perched high on the slopes. "Every day of the year, I prepare myself for this sunny July day when I will climb slowly up as far as the station for the funicular railway from Saint-Luc to the Weisshorn. It's my summer rapture!" he added with a glowing smile. "In the old days, I used to do this climb in an hour. I didn't even look where I was putting my feet, and I flew up to the summit. Nowadays, it takes me three hours to get there. I look at my feet while I'm walking, and take a newfound pleasure in noticing things I never used to see, like the flowers lining the way. I greet them by their names: hello, blue gentian; hello, yellow anemone; hello, snow-colored forget-me-not. I often stop to listen to the cool sound of the waterfalls rushing down the slope, and the youthful sound of the big bells that hang round the necks of the black cows — you know, the ones known as queens, which are trained to fight. I stop and I gaze upon all this beauty. I breathe in the wonderfully pure air, and I repeat to myself inwardly: thank you, thank you! And then, a little higher up" — he pointed to the path, which struggled across loose stones amid a carpet of dazzlingly red dwarf rhododendrons — "do you see those pyramids of stones which people have created spontaneously? Well, they are a sort of chorten, like they have in Nepal. People pile stones one on top of another as a sign of gratitude. Every summer, when I come here, I lay my own stone and I thank Life, with a capital *L,* the Living One, that I am still here, in good health, and capable of such happiness!"

"May I ask how old you are?" I ventured.

"I'm seventy-nine. I've always loved walking, and I think it's wonderful that I can still go on doing it, but nowadays I see my walking in a quite different way. I see it from the inside. I walk profoundly. When I was young, it was physical performance that counted. I barely saw the landscape. Now I dwell in each second; my eyes are in a permanent state of ecstasy. I am endlessly intoxicated by scents. There is rather a difficult stretch just before you get to the Weisshorn, with blocks of limestone strewn across the path, and each year I wonder if I shall be able to get past. But if I go gently, carefully — and knowing that I'm almost there makes it easier — I think that I shall manage it this year, too."

The old gentleman stood up. He had a handsome, bronzed face, marked with lines of determination. I still remember his words and his smile, and I have attempted to pass them on to everyone who, like me, would like to be able to climb mountain paths at his age, and with an equally light heart.

## Meditation, Simplified

When you have grown old, newness always comes from the inside. A new sensibility, a kind of sensual perception, becomes keener with age and mysteriously increases while the body diminishes. Karlfried Dürckheim talks about "opening the Organ which permits the perception of Reality, in the heart of which flows the inexhaustible spring of being, independent of the specific modalities of existence."[10] It is really up to those who are advancing in age to enter into a relationship with their inner self. The establishment of this relationship can be accomplished in several ways, and I would like to mention a few here.

The first is quite simply to "let go." Incredible results can happen — for instance, forcing oneself to breathe out through a painful part of the body, what Durkheim calls "the antinatural act," rather than the opposite, which holds in the breath and resists against pain, stiffening and blocking the aching part.

The road to deep relaxation, "the great Detachment," is to breathe correctly. This should not be regarded merely as a way of taking in and expelling air, but as a great rhythm, to which we open and close ourselves, give ourselves and then pull back, offer ourselves and collect our thoughts. First, one must focus on letting go when exhaling, by relaxing at the top, sitting down, and positioning the pelvis so that breathing remains effortless.[11]

It is thought that meditation for ten minutes each day for two or three months can help lower blood pressure by two points without any medication. The process consists of closing one's eyes and breathing deeply, starting from the top of the lungs down to the abdomen (as yogis do). This slows down the beating of the heart and causes facial muscles to relax and smile like a Buddha. Daily meditation for ten minutes is the equivalent of several hours of sleep, and accessible to all.[12]

Positioning yourself in this way, occupying the breath, enables you to become aware of the body you are, and as you make the breath travel through the body, you feel all your tensions unwind. With practice, you feel deeply but gently moved by a strange feeling, and reach a state of wholesome contentment. These sensations reveal a new inner space. An elderly person's sterile internal space may come to life again: this does not mean it has rejuvenated, but represents an awakening to a different Life, a timeless state outside the realm of action.[13]

Places where people meditate, whether they are Christians or Buddhists, are also very popular with senior citizens. The "work of growing old" adapts well to a practice that consists of sitting down, creating emptiness, and experiencing silence. As growing old consists partly of detaching oneself and accepting a degree of solitude, it is understandable that many senior citizens model themselves on spiritual people. "Every day, I make myself spend half an hour in silence. Whenever I can, I go to the Lady Chapel at Saint-Gervais Church in Paris. Because it is a place of silence, it helps me to enter my inner crypt. I feel good there. I await the moment joyfully, I can tell you, because then I feel light. I feel that I am not in danger of anything and that I can die in peace. There is this place inside me that belongs to me as I sit there, just holding my breath, with this life inside and around me!" a friend tells me; and indeed the thought of growing old does not seem to worry her.

## Rediscovering the Body

If we could instruct all elderly people on how to perceive the "body they are," much of the suffering linked to the "body they have" could be overcome. This training demands time, attention, and receptiveness, but these three qualities are not at all incompatible with old age. It is a matter of exercising, developing, and sharpening one's perception. Immense joy lies in store for those who discover a private universe previously unknown to them. Their exterior body may be in ruins, but their interior body is more vibrant and alive than ever.

If we let go in this way, a new form of sensuality becomes apparent; one in which hearing and sight become less important, and touch often benefits. "Perhaps more than ever, the skin becomes a place of exchange and of pleasure," writes Jérôme Pélissier.[14] The present acquires a new value "in which the sensations, thoughts, and emotions of the moment are more fully savored. There is pleasure in feeling motionless, in existing." Jérôme Pélissier goes on to talk about being "reunited" with himself. "The mind derives its food from within, from what it has accumulated during life."[15] He has discovered that the essential content — made up of thoughts, emotions, and dreams — was present as early as childhood. It brings back memories so that we can better "understand in depth the fundamental reality that we have lived, beyond our awareness of the initial experience."[16] The point of this is to search for the meaning of the life one has lived; old age offers the time and mental space to do so.

Hermann Hesse invites us to turn our attention to "the treasury of images we retain in our memory after a long life," to leaf cautiously through "the great album of our life," and to note "how wondrous and good it is to withdraw from pursuit, from this mad race, and to attain the *vita contemplativa.*"[17]

In the "garden of old age," patience blossoms. "We become peaceable and tolerant. The more our desire to intervene and act diminishes, the more growth we see in our ability to observe, to listen to nature as well as to mankind.

"It is only as we grow old that we notice that beauty is rare, that we understand the miracle of a flower blooming amid ruins and gunfire and the survival of literary works amid the newspapers and the stock market lists."[18]

## Disability as an Advantage

This enjoyment in existence is perhaps even more accessible to those whose pace of life has slowed down, or who are forced into immobility. Earlier on, when I talked about fear of dependency, I mentioned the words of the bedridden professor who said that he appreciated the tree he saw through his window as he never had before.

Instead of rebelling against the exhaustion, the slowing down, and the fatigue that affects us when we grow older, why don't we accept it all, and allow ourselves to be borne along by the current? Why not stretch out and rest, as suggested by Ram Dass: "We should ask ourselves in moments of fatigue whether slowing down may not be a message to attend to the moment — to be with it . . . to taste it . . . to embrace it; a way of making us take time, finally, to tend to what's here now. Are these changes in energy a sign of how we could be evolving, quieting down, becoming more reflective? In India, this is the time when people look to give up their responsibilities and turn to cultivation of the soul."[19]

Ram Dass, who was left hemiplegic following a cerebral hemorrhage, says that after accepting his situation, he is much happier than he was before. "This troubles some of the people around me. They have told me that I should fight to walk again, but I don't know if I want to walk. I'm sitting — that's where I am. I'm peaceful like this and I am grateful to the people who care for me."[20]

One of my friends, the writer Gilles Farcet, met this captivating individual eleven years earlier, and asked him what he would do if he ever became disabled and forced into inactivity. Ram Dass replied:

It would certainly be very good. I

would become increasingly calm, would immerse myself in the depths, to the point where I would become a sort of presence to whom people could come to warm themselves. I have met a lot of old people who exude a real presence. They never say anything and are content just to be there. I met one of these men a few weeks ago in Nepal. He was physically so diminished and yet spiritually so present, so radiant. . . . Perhaps I would be in a position to make a gift of such a presence to other people. I hope so, in any case. God willing, I hope my spirit will never lose the feeling of contemplation that has been inspired in me by the precariousness of all things, by my passion for metamorphoses, my acceptance of death, my will to be reborn! Let us allow things to happen smoothly, moving from one step to the next, from one space to another, and let us remain alert, always ready to experience something new.[21]

## The Still Point

In his writings, Frans Veldman draws attention to what he calls the "still point," an internal point of tranquillity that one can learn to detect and listen to. Karlfried

Dürckheim talks about "touching one's Being." Here I have given the example of two original Western approaches, for they appropriate something that has long been the prerogative of the Orient: the promotion of inaction, silence, and calm.

"I am beginning to understand the pleasure that the old experience when they sit on a bench for hours in the shade of a plane tree, doing nothing, gazing into the distance, silent, motionless, their hands folded," François Mitterrand told me in the last months of his life. He had been so active, yet he understood the virtues of "nonaction." Old people may do nothing, but they are. Many of our contemporaries regard doing nothing as a defect or a calamity when inactivity is imposed. Few people realize that by simply being, sitting peacefully, one can fully savor the present, and one has a chance "to perceive what gleams in our innermost depths, 'something' whose touch is extremely light and subtle, but which is full of the quality we call Numinous."[22] Karlfried Dürckheim attempts thus to explain this experience of nonaction, but one senses that it is so ineffable, it is extremely difficult to make agitated people like us understand the happiness one can feel in simply being:

Everything around him is linked to the Infinite, and mysteriously the waves ebb and flow between the old man who sits outside his door and the distance into which he gazes, whether it be the sea, the plains, the forest, the mountains or the sky; it may also be a tall tree outside his window or the wall of his bedroom . . . and even the darkness of his dying eyes. His way of looking turns what he sees into a form of the Infinite. From this ebb and flow of Infinity inside him, he derives his Peace, a radiant and perfect Peace, a blessed Peace. Is he happy? There are no words to describe this state, to describe what may happen then; but there, where he is sitting, there is "something" whose fulfillment he experiences.[23]

# THE LAST JOYS OF OLD AGE

The philosopher and poet Jean-Louis Chrétien recently published an essay on joy, that emotion which makes the heart swell. "In joy, everything is more expansive because I grow larger, and I grow larger because the world opens wider." Joy brings about a veritable "growth of space and existence."[1]

The exciting thing about Jean-Louis Chrétien's work is the way in which he describes his experience of joy and explains how it alters his perception of his own body — which may shrink or enlarge according to whether it is aerated or asphyxiated by his state of mind. When we have a heavy heart — when we are sad, depressed, or anxious — we feel confined in our body, as if something were squeezing it tightly. We wish we could die. "But if a smile, a piece of good news, or a happy event comes along, then one becomes bigger than the world, one is an ocean, a starry immensity — one 'overflows with joy,' as the saying goes."[2] When the heart swells, the whole of our existence acquires another dimension. "We breathe more deeply, and our body — which just a moment before was withdrawn and huddled in a corner — suddenly sits up straight and quivers with activity. We want to jump, leap, dance, for we are more alive and inhabiting a vaster space," Chrétien writes.[3]

Joy makes our hearts swell, and does not cost anyone anything, or deprive anybody of space. We can now understand more clearly how this experience of the heart revolutionizes the private life of an elderly person, who may be weak and vulnerable, bedridden, or confined to a wheelchair. For years, I have been telling carers taking my training courses that the power of a word, a gesture, or a smile is immeasurable. By bringing joy into the heart of the person who receives that word, gesture, or smile, they give that person space.

Jean-Pierre Van Rillaer manages the Résidence Simonis, a retirement home north of Brussels that houses 134 residents from underprivileged backgrounds at extremely low cost. Self-sufficient residents live side by side with others who are completely dependent or who suffer from dementia.

The home also has a few younger residents, all severely handicapped due to traumatic injuries, who have nowhere else to go. In other words, this place is a microcosm of all the world's miseries. I accompanied Jean-Pierre on his rounds of the cafeteria during mealtime. As soon as he entered the vast hall, the residents drew themselves up straight. It must be said that this forty-eight-year-old man is handsome and charismatic, and there is no doubt that everyone there instantly detected his benevolent, even luminous, presence. He went from one person to the next smiling broadly, exchanging affectionate words, and kissing one or two of the women. No, I was not dreaming! I felt truly overwhelmed as I saw joy flash across sad, tired eyes, and I thought about Jean-Louis Chrétien's "spacious joy": "Where previously every thing had seemed closed, a path opens up."[4] There is no doubt that, just for a moment, everyone there felt their hearts swell and their bodies expand. I am not sure if Jean-Pierre is really aware of the miracles he works, and perhaps it is better that way, but I do know that he is happy in his work.

Returning to the treatment room, we talked about the joy I had seen appearing on the residents' faces. From the outside, these residents seemed engulfed in a sort of night, doing almost nothing from morning till evening. What did they experience? Were they bored? Were they waiting for something? Jean-Pierre asked me why people should always have to be active, always doing something, in order to "be." Perhaps if the residents did not exist in this twilight state, they would not be receptive to joy, or capable of feeling it when it was brought to them by another person.

## Our Inner Garden

A friend of mine, Annick de Souzenelle, who is more than eighty years old, tells me that in Hebrew a single word, *guil*, designates both age and joy. This is exciting: Hebrew has created a relationship between the elderly and someone who is drunk with joy. "Old age is the time when one acquires joy," she says. "However, the 'old man' — that is, one's past identity — must be put to death during one's life. The many losses linked to advancing age are keys that trip and unlock the heart, and one then enters ever-deeper levels of consciousness. Upon returning home to one's inner world, there is no more loneliness, for a link has been forged to the divine. Without this, old age is tragic, and the loneliness abominable."

These words became clearer to me one day as I sat down beside an old friend from the île d'Yeu on a little bench propped against a fisherman's hut, looking out to sea. My friend asked me: "How can anyone be bored?" A thousand times he has come to sit on that bench, which overlooks the rocks of the Raie-Profonde, and watch the sunrise. He never tires of it. The sun is never the same twice, the light changes constantly, and so does the color of the rocks. On that particular morning the air was especially mild, and I caught him with his eyes closed, completely absorbed in feeling the sun's first rays on his age-lined face. "How can people be bored when they are old?" he repeated. Then he showed me the news-paper article he had just read about a book entitled *The Courage to Grow Old.* "Listen!" he said. "This is the time to sing, dance, and play, for as long as we can. It is the time to marvel at nature, which will still be there when we are gone; to enjoy the sun, which will still be here when it no longer warms us; to make the most of the grandchildren, who will still be around when we are not." And listen to this! "Sooner or later, a mo-ment comes in all our lives when our prior-ity will be to cultivate our inner garden, to till it more deeply, and dig up its unexpected fruits; to follow the example of the monk or the cloistered nun, the solitary sage or the old men of the village, calmly conversing on the bench that leans against the church. There is nothing about this that resembles desertion or emptiness. It is merely *being more* internally and *doing less* externally."[5] (Italics added.)

I love these moments of philosophy. We went on to discuss the death of Paul Ricoeur, a man who gave a lot of thought to old age, and who identified two principal dangers: sadness and boredom. "On the subject of sadness, what can be controlled is not the emotion itself," he used to say. "It is the consent to feel sadness, what the Fathers of the Church called *acedia*." When it came to boredom, he made a distinction: "There is the boredom of the child who says: 'I don't know what to do'; then there is the boredom of someone who has lived a long time and who says to him- or herself: 'I've seen all this before!' " It is this boredom that emanates from so many old people in our institutions as they wait sadly for death. I wondered, is there a way to ward off this plague? "Yes," he said. "Be attentive and open to everything new that happens. Remain capable of what Descartes called admiration. To me, that is the wisdom of old age. I hope to be capable of it for as long as God gives me strength."[6]

## The Ability to Marvel

To be filled with admiration and wonderment is a joy that is within everyone's grasp, and one that is widely shared. Some writers in their eighties talk movingly about this ability to marvel as one of the "blessings of old age."[7] It is:

the miracle of seeing that here we are, at this very moment, still alive, and coming and going, both welcoming and welcomed, feeling desire and desired, and feeling and tasting and gazing upon all things that endure around us!

The miracle of thinking that, weighed down with years, we have managed to increase our burden of life, enriching and amplifying it . . . and that we have overcome so many obstacles, parried so many blows, confronted envy, hatred, and adversity, suffered bereavements and losses and come through wars, riots, rebellions, catastrophes . . . and find ourselves, here and now, on this old, enduring earth . . . so that at this very moment, though our eyes may be veiled and darkened, we can turn in delight toward the warm brightness of the sun, catch the sudden rain showers in our teeth, however shaky or loose they may be, watch the wondrous clouds perform their giant acrobatics, and discover that we are entirely ready, each evening, to hail the silent, luxuriant sparkle of the stars.[8]

Benoîte Groult was intrigued by this sensitivity to the beauty of things, "the tiniest miracles and the greatest spectacles coming together to bring tears to my eyes: the blue of the plumbagos, the flight of the cranes in *Le peuple migrateur* (a film called *Winged Migration*), the rosebush I called Cézanne which I planted last year in an unpromising corner, without much hope, and which provided me with its first bright-hued red and yellow rose in November."[9]

This ability to marvel, to contemplate, is a form of compensation. If we listen to all the elderly people who praise this passive virtue, we will begin to believe that old age is the time we have been dreaming of, a time that will open our eyes to the world. We have lived, seen, thought, felt, and endured so much — an infinite sum of things! It is as if our egos were being polished, worn away, and rendered transparent, the way the sea wears away the mother-of-pearl from shells. A year before her death, a writer friend declared that old people become so transparent, you can see life through them, and they in turn see beyond life's objects.

Poets of every era have sought to express this extreme sensitivity linked to the vulnerability of old age and the proximity of death. For example, Hermann Hesse tells us that once when he was standing beside the fire, cutting wood on a mild, still day, he became aware of his extreme proximity to death:

I saw the thing coming: an imperceptible, lukewarm breeze suddenly began to blow, a simple breath, and the leaves that had been spared for so long took flight in their hundreds and thousands; silent, light, docile, weary of their perseverance, weary of their resistance and their bravery. Within a few minutes, that which had held on and resisted for five or six months succumbed to a mere nothing, a breath: the end-time had sounded, and bitter perseverance was no longer necessary. The leaves dispersed, floated away at the whim of the wind, smiling, consenting, without a fight. . . . What had revealed this surprising, pathetic sight to me? . . . Was it a warning

aimed at the old man I was, commanding me, too, to flutter up and then fall?[10]

# KNOWING HOW TO DIE

The older we become, the closer we are to death. If we have not become accustomed to thinking about it, to meditating on this final end, it is highly likely that we will be overcome by anxiety. The generations before ours experienced metaphysical fears linked to their beliefs and religious education. People were afraid of purgatory and hell, and I have accompanied a great many old people to the threshold of death, people who told me about their dreams of the Last Judgment. They were terrified. Today, fear of the afterlife has been replaced by a diffuse anxiety and by depression. Our generation, the generation of the aging population, no longer asks what awaits us beyond death. The muffled anguish that grips us seems to derive from an impossible or painful confrontation with the balance sheet of our lives. "In the face of death," the theologian Maurice Zundel writes, "one becomes aware of the fact that life could have been something immense, prodigious, and creative, but now it is too late and life stands out in full detail against the background of the immense regret one feels for what was not accomplished. At this moment, precisely because life has not been fully accomplished, death looms up like an abyss."[1]

This fear of the abyss grips a person who at the end of his life realizes that he has missed out on what really mattered. Maurice Zundel exposes one of the reasons for this fear: the prospect of definitively passing away and dissolving into nothingness is all the more terrifying when one does not really know why one has lived. This should give us an understanding of the importance of any words exchanged between a dying person and those who are at his or her bedside. A person can pass away without dying completely if she knows that she will leave behind some words of peace, gratitude, life. "Death puts an end to life, but not to relationships," said an old man on the threshold of death. "You go on living in the hearts of those whom you have touched and nurtured during your lifetime."[2]

When we feel that our essence survives, if only in the memory of those we love, death is no longer frightening. The psychotherapist

Marie-Louise von Franz told me about a dream that one of her patients had when she was close to death.[3] This woman reported that she had dreamed of a devastating fire. She saw flames completely destroy a field of wheat, but — to her great surprise — one tree remained intact in the middle of the field, and from its branches hung a golden apple. The Swiss therapist, a pupil of Jung, then explained how the dream had reassured her patient by showing her that her essential being, her Self, symbolized by the golden apple, could not be destroyed. As we grow older and become more aware of our own Self, we are also less afraid of dying: for, as Spinoza put it, we experience the fact that we are eternal.

Almost all old people experience the fear of dying badly, unless they spend their last days among people who have undertaken to care for them and be with them right to the end. Consequently, it is rare for elderly people to be afraid of death where palliative care is practiced, and where there is a culture of accompanying the dying. But everywhere else, this fear torments our elderly. They are afraid that they will end their lives in extreme suffering or in terrible, interminable death throes, bedridden and with tubes sticking out of their bodies;

or that they will die alone, gripped by unbearable anguish.[4] They are afraid of the slow deterioration that precedes death, the weakening, and the dependency that forces us to entrust our bodies to the care of others. They are afraid of being mistreated by indifferent or brutal carers, exacerbating the feeling that they have become insignificant. The prospect of these experiences, combined with a lack of trust in other people's humanity and the fear of becoming a burden, lead many elderly people to think about anticipating their deaths and some form of assisted suicide.

Senior citizens sometimes decide to put an end to their days when they fall victim to Alzheimer's disease. The prospect of living through their own inexorable physical and mental collapse is too much for them.

I remember a meeting I had with the astrophysicist Hubert Reeves in 1999. He confided in me that he was afraid of dying, imagining that it would be a terrible experience. He told me about a very intelligent and admirable friend who had become completely mad, aggressive, and hateful at the end of her life. This vision haunted him. How could a person be transformed in such a way and leave such an image with his or her loved ones? "It is better to anticipate one's death than to inflict such a sight upon those who admire and love you," he told me.

Suicide among the elderly is a subject that remains relatively taboo. But the number of senior citizens committing suicide is continually rising.

Some of the senior citizens I know are thinking — apparently quite serenely — about the possibility of putting an end to their days at the point when they feel that their lives are no longer worth living. Others, however, say that they are quite determined to live right to the end, whatever happens. These are the words of senior citizens who are in good health; but when responding to situations they have witnessed, they all envisage a more or less terrifying future.

Without wishing to overgeneralize, I would say that those who have witnessed difficult deaths among their nearest and dearest are unwilling to face similar situations under any circumstances, and would prefer to anticipate their own deaths; on the other hand, those who have accompanied a dying loved one in favorable circumstances — even if that person was dependent or suffering from dementia — are planning to see their lives through to the end.

I have attempted to understand what differentiates these groups. A fashion seems to be developing among senior citizens: to live in good health for as long as possible and as well as possible, enjoying their old age, and then, when the prospect of a life of dependency and the attendant loss of mental faculties hovers into view, they plan to put an end to their lives or ask a doctor to do so. Allowing themselves to decline slowly is out of the question.

I have been too fond of running, climbing, skiing, and driving to accept giving in to the constraints of a Zimmer frame [walker]. I have been too fond of the taste of wine and single malts, and vodka's perfume of eternal snow to see a plastic bottle beside my plate, filled with a colorless liquid devoid of smell or taste. I have been too fond of kneeling in the garden, breathing in the scent of the earth, and digging and planting and pruning; I have been too fond of the lofty sun at its zenith, too fond of swimming in the icy ocean and rambling on the moors to doze in the shade in a garden, with a broad-brimmed hat on my head and a blanket on my legs, waiting for night to fall . . . and go to bed![5]

So writes Benoîte Groult, who says that because she loves life, she would like to leave it in good time. How does Groult know what a very elderly person really feels as he or she dozes under a blanket? How can she appreciate the private experiences of someone who, with the aid of a walker, can still go outside to breathe in the spring air? Perhaps she simply could not imagine herself in the place of her sister, who was lapsing — perhaps not as painfully as all that — into Alzheimer's disease.

There is currently a demand in France for a law to decriminalize assisted suicide: a movement that reveals the depth of our generation's fear of growing old unhappily, of dying badly, and — quite simply — of death. In 1997 the state of Oregon passed the Death with Dignity Act. This initiative was followed by the state of Washington in 2009, and allows terminally ill patients access to doses of lethal medicine to terminate their lives prematurely. It is no surprise, then, that in the United States, a large number of people aged over seventy-five have completed living wills and assigned power of attorney to relatives in accordance with the Patient Self-Determination Act of 1990. Although the laws on certain medical procedures vary from state to state, the idea of being able to "speak" one's wishes when incapacitated remains comforting for many. By signing a living will requesting that their wish not to suffer is respected, that they not be kept alive by disproportionate and artificial methods, and that they be given active help to die, these individuals hope that their wish to die "with dignity" will be taken seriously.

The French law entitled "Patients' Rights and the End of Life" now guarantees that a request not to be kept alive by artificial means and treatments will be respected. An elderly person who does not wish to go on living cannot get a doctor to kill him, but can oblige the doctor to let him die. How? By halting all treatment that is designed to keep him alive. And if a patient refuses to eat, his refusal will be respected. When we think of all the elderly people who used to be forced to live by being fed through a gastric tube, sometimes being strapped to the bars of the bed so that they could not tear out their drip, we can appreciate the progress that this new law represents. But our senior citizens feel that this law does not go far enough. They would like to have the means to control their own death, to decide the day and the hour, and they reject the idea of a progressive descent into death.

"Seeing oneself die by inches, how horrible!" I have often heard people say, as if gently passing away were the equivalent of torture. It is clear from listening to them that they have had no experience of affectionately and serenely accompanying their loved ones, of sharing a meditative vigil at the dying person's bedside.

An extremely lively debate has sprung up in the Netherlands regarding the assisted suicide of elderly people. We should remember that euthanasia is permitted in the Netherlands, but only under certain conditions, and only for sick people who are experiencing unbearable suffering. An elderly person who is tired of living, for example, cannot request euthanasia.

This is why an eighty-five-year-old retired judge, Huibert Drion, argued in favor of assisted suicide, which remains prohibited in Holland. He said that when he becomes housebound and no longer takes pleasure in the pastimes he used to enjoy, he would like to have the right to die — even if he was not suffering from illness.

Els Borst, who was the Dutch minister of health, well-being, and sport from 1994 to 2002, has spoken out in favor of marketing and distributing a lethal pill — now known as "the Drion pill" — to individuals suffering from Alzheimer's disease. She believes it is the right solution, and also advocates assisted suicide for very elderly people who are not ill but who no longer want to live and yet do not die.

Judge Drion suggested that this "last wish pill" should be distributed to all elderly people, leaving it up to them to decide when they would take it, but this proposal caused an outcry. Members of parliament demanded a safety net to protect the elderly from the risk of abuse by those around them. Should doctors be made responsible for delivering this pill? Many doctors are violently opposed to the idea. They feel that being tired of life does not justify such an act, and that the administration of a lethal substance to a person who is not ill is no task for a doctor. As they see it, this is not a medical issue but a social one, for which society should be responsible.

As yet, the Drion pill still has not received approval, although a request for a patent has been lodged with the European Patent Office in Munich. It seems that it cannot progress any further as long as it remains contrary to the European Convention on the Rights of Man. A telephone call to the Dutch embassy confirmed that this issue is no longer on the agenda.

Elsewhere in the world, the idea of manufacturing a lethal pill for the most elderly members of society is making progress. At an international conference on the right to die with dignity, held in Toronto, Canada, the Australian doctor Philip Nitschke announced that a group of senior citizens with an average age of eighty had succeeded in manufacturing a suicide pill that they could use one day if they needed to. The majority had no specific knowledge of chemistry and were in good health. They passed themselves off as amateur ornithologists and concealed their laboratory on a farm in New South Wales. The doctor explained to them how to manufacture a lethal pill, and it took them a year to achieve success. It is currently being analyzed in an Australian laboratory. Dr. Nitschke defends the idea that in countries where assisted suicide is illegal, the law could be circumvented by helping individuals to manufacture a suicide pill without outside help. This would give them an opportunity to kill themselves without the risk of anyone being charged with a legal offense. However, he added that he thought the majority of these senior citizens would never take their pills, for all they want is to know that it is within reach if need be. It would seem that other senior citizens have already signed up to manufacture their own "pill of last resort."

Are elderly people who ask us to help them die really asking us for something else? What if we recognize that they still have a place among us, if we are still willing to show them consideration and respect? We are responsible for this time that they have left to live, and which should therefore be respected.

At a time when compassionate murder is referred to so easily as an expression of our humanity, it takes much more courage to question the deeper motives behind this request for death. Too often, it reveals a failure on our part to be a friend or relative to this lonely old person. We all know how effectively a sign, a gesture, a word, or a direct, friendly look can drive away loneliness.

I knew of a biologist who committed suicide at the end of her life. She planned it, she said beforehand, because she always planned everything. When a journalist asked her one day if she was depriving her children of the end of her life, she replied: "Deprive? What does that mean? What would it give to them? They have their own lives, their cares; they have their own families."

These words reveal more than just a woman's simple desire to control her own death. They suggest that her end concerned no one but her, and that she had nothing to give to others by living her life to its end. In saying so, she expressed what thousands of elderly people think today: How can the last moments of an old person contribute anything? Are we still good for something when we can no longer do anything — when our tired, sick bodies lie helplessly in our beds?

How sad that elderly people do not realize that by experiencing their death in the presence of their loved ones, they communicate something precious. They show their loved ones that human beings are capable of accomplishing this last act of life.

Over the years, as I accompanied individuals in their last moments of life, I came to believe that this "dying time," however slow it might be, had a meaning. My proximity to the dying enabled me to appreciate the sheer extent of their wait. How can we die without saying good-bye to those who matter, without hearing them speak the words of love that give us the strength to let go, and without feeling that we are at peace with them? How can we die without leaving those who remain with a word, a gesture, or

a look to console them through the separation and help them to live; without giving
them a final benediction? I use the term
*benediction* — which means "good words"
— deliberately, to stress the importance of
these liberating words. We must stop thinking that only a lethal substance can "deliver"
the dying person. There is too much evidence in favor of a quite different kind of
deliverance.

I have had the good fortune to see old
people put their affairs in order, gather their
families around, talk to them, and bless
them, and then, after this final farewell,
return to silence and await death. This was
never long in coming, for these farewell rituals have a real symbolic power.

Such scenes are rare today, and yet they
represent a true process of handing over to
those who remain. I have several of these
farewell scenes locked away in my memory,
and from time to time I tell myself that at
the moment of my own death, I would like
to remember them. Is that not dying with
dignity?

How can we cast off our mooring ropes
when the time has come? It is certainly not
easy to think serenely about how one's life
will end. There is so much uncertainty. No

one knows where or when or how it will happen — and there is the difficulty of trusting oneself and trusting others. An elderly person's request to end it all is often a way of testing those around him, of provoking the other person: the doctor, the caregiver, or the relative. What he expects is reassurance that he has not been abandoned.

If we "work at growing old," if we accept the progressive loss of certain faculties while at the same time discovering others, we may achieve a transformation of the self accompanied by a form of self-confidence. Growing old chips away at one's self-esteem, but it also opens the heart. Why shouldn't this opening up be a viaticum for death?

I have given a great deal of thought to the way I would like to die. I have planned everything, although I am perfectly aware of the limits of such an exercise. For death may perhaps seize me in a way I cannot imagine. But if I am fortunate enough to live until I am very old, and if a moment comes when — like so many others before me — I feel that I am deteriorating to the point where I am becoming a burden to those I love, I would not want my death to be stolen from me, nor for someone to decide in my place that the moment has come. I hope I am sufficiently clear-headed to know when it is time to go. But do not imagine that I am thinking of suicide in the proper sense of the word, nor of encumbering someone else with the excessive burden of performing euthanasia. I would like to have the courage to bring myself to death, as my mother-in-law did — an amazing experience that I recounted in my previous book *Nous ne nous sommes pas dit au revoir* (We Didn't Say Good-bye).[6]

Feeling that life was beginning to desert her and that her memory was starting to fail, and having lost all taste for food, she decided one day to go to bed, to stop taking nourishment, and to wait for death. It was a considered and irrevocable decision, for she did not want to deteriorate, or to end her life in an institution. Nor was it a fleeting attack of depression. She was not sad but simply weary of living. My husband, her son, Christopher, decided to respect her wishes. At that time, he could have been prosecuted for failing to assist a person in danger, but nowadays it is legal to respect such a refusal to eat. He organized regular visits from a doctor and a home-care nurse so that she would not suffer and would receive treatment until the end, and so that she could be given assistance with washing herself and with her intimate needs as she began to weaken. Christopher and his friends and neighbors were with her right to the end. It took her two months to die. It sometimes seemed a long time to her, but at no point did she wish for someone to speed up the process, for she did not want to impose any kind of violent action on anyone. She wanted to pass away gently. When Christopher asked her what she was doing all day, she replied: "Loving, I suppose."

That is how I would like to die: as in *The Ballad of Narayama,* in which an old woman walks resolutely toward death because the time has come for her to leave and to make room for others. Around her are people who accompany her and respect her choice, who give her what people are so bad at giving to the dying: the permission to die.[7]

# CONCLUSION

The sage of the Black Forest, Karlfried
Dürckheim, said of old age that its meaning
was not so much "a catastrophic end as the
veritable marriage of man with his eternal
face." He explained that this presupposes
that we plunge our roots into a reality that
exists beyond the dichotomy of young and
old, and that we awaken to our inner self,
letting go more profoundly than ever. Hence
a person who says "yes to old age" attains
something "absolutely brand-new," and "the
veil that separates him from the invisible
world can become transparent in the extreme." Instead of being a poison to the
whole family, adds Karlfried Dürckheim,
"this old man is a beacon to those around
him, he secretly attracts others with his radiance, and he is admired and loved for the
unspoken qualities that emanate from him.
He has found true youthfulness."[1]

As we step onto the banks of the third age,

we may now have all the keys to growing old positively. Medicine and science will help us. We will take care of our health, taking part in sport and remaining useful to our society, and retaining links with other people. We will successfully control our interests and defend them, and devise solutions that enable us all to remain united. All of this will help, but the strength of our vitality and our joie de vivre as we age will depend upon how we have worked at growing old.

By introducing this concept of "work," I want to emphasize the effort of detachment and alertness that is demanded of us at this stage in our lives. We must let go: let go of our past, become reconciled with ourselves, and accept that we will be diminished in one respect in order to grow in another. This is what Jung called the "process of individuation." By abandoning outmoded, selfish pretensions, and carrying out this work of detachment, we will return to a deeper dimension of our being. Jung calls it the Self; Dürckheim, the essential being; and Saint Paul, the inner man. Each of us, in our own way, can identify this hitherto unsuspected strength, this urge that forever reaches out toward what is new. That is why Karlfried Dürckheim talks about "real youthfulness."

There is no other way of growing old well than to move toward this radiance, this youthfulness of heart. Throughout this book, I have attempted to arouse this desire in my contemporaries, the senior citizens of the baby boom. I set myself the challenge of taking a long, hard look at what frightens us so much about old age. I have tried not to prettify things but not to overdarken them either under the pretext of being clear-sighted. I have attempted to follow the common theme given to me by the respectable and enviable citizens of Okinawa: "The warmth of the heart prevents your body from rusting." Wherever we grow old and whatever our circumstances, if we can maintain this energy of the heart, it is capable of transforming us and of transforming the way we look at the world.

Letting go is vital. But we are surrounded by people who grow old in a state of bitterness and rebellion. One old friend, who has just turned eighty, recently complained that he felt as though he were involved in a shipwreck.

"The mechanism which life has chosen in order to bring about death is unacceptable," he told me. "The fact that we are forced to lose our strength, to look on helplessly as our selves diminish, is the greatest reproach I can deliver to Creation." Laughing, I replied that Woody Allen is wiser than he is, for he has nothing against the fact of growing old, "since nobody has found a better way of not dying young."

Until we stop fixating on reproach, we will not be able to attain a light, happy, free old age. This is, however, possible. As we have seen, many people are experiencing it — even in situations we fear, like dependency; or in places that frighten us, like retirement homes. The path that leads there is a path of consciousness and confidence.

It is strange that at both ends of life, nature allows us a time when we are dependent on others, such that we have no other choice than to be carried, trustingly. This is what we all experienced when we came into the world and during the first years of our lives, but we were not aware of it. At the end of our lives, many of us are in the same condition once again, partially or totally dependent upon other humans, or sufficiently diminished to have need of assistance. But this second time we are aware of it, and it is up to us either to reject this state, to withdraw into ourselves and suffer, or to accept it. In acceptance, we may then have the most profound experience it is possible to have — that of abandoning ourselves to others and agreeing to receive their help. It is when we can no longer "do" anything that we can gain access to the supreme freedom, that of "being," the freedom of entrusting ourselves to the world's kindness, which then manifests itself, as always, through the humanity and compassion of those around us.

The philosopher Emmanuel Levinas understood this concept perfectly. In *Ethics and Infinity,* he links humanity and vulnerability by describing the moment when one encounters another person's face. Levinas means that when a "strong" (i.e., not vulnerable) person sees a vulnerable person's face, he recognizes that person's vulnerability and this taps into his humanity and feeling of responsibility to help the vulnerable one. The vulnerable face is a face that overwhelms us with its nudity, arouses in us a sense of infinite responsibility. For unless we are perverted or mad, how could we not protect someone who in his extreme weakness abandons himself to our hands?

During a conversation I had about old age with Bertrand Vergely, he reconsidered this unexpected ontological stroke of fortune, which is offered to those who have experienced all the ages of life and have now arrived at the stage of spiritual poverty. This is the age in which, as François Mitterrand put it so well, the body is "broken on the edge of infinity,"[2] and one loses almost every faculty. It is an age of helplessness and vulnerability: an age in which the only thing left is to accept everything that happens with an open heart.

Growing old offers us this opportunity to experience what the Stoics called true freedom, the freedom of allowing things to happen, allowing things to be, of putting oneself in the hands of the universe. Many more people than we imagine are happy to experience this diminution in old age, because it liberates them. "They have agreed to experience their limits, without complaint, and are like children. They look at the world around them in wonderment, as though it were a gift, a miracle, a game. They are no longer involved in reality. In a way they are experiencing the nonaction of the Tao," Bertrand said. It is an immense paradox: old age, with all its handicaps, is a time of immense freedom. This is why elderly people who live their old age in this way exert a certain attraction on others. He continued: "People come to see them because they are radiant in their simplicity

261

and their gentleness, because they pass on a kind of 'disengagement,' a kind of lightness or humor. They help others to gain height or distance.

"Finally, life is well constructed, and this time of old age has been given to us for a reason. It contains its own mystery," Bertrand concluded, as if in response to the words of that eighty-year-old friend who did not share his point of view. "The impossibility we face obliges us to let go in a way that all sages seek to do. Life has given us a key, that of accepting our helplessness; for helplessness does not lead us to tragedy, but to lightness of heart and joy."

As I left my friend the philosopher, I thought again of the last words of an old woman of ninety-two half an hour before her death. It was many years ago, when I was working as a psychologist at the bedsides of the dying. Her eyes filled with fire, she seized my hand and, gripping it forcefully, entrusted me with her last message: "My child, don't be afraid of anything. Live! Live every bit of life that is given to you! For everything, everything, is a gift from God." As I write these words, her words, I can still feel the energy she communicated to me as she spoke them. I can feel it as strongly as if it has just happened: proof that what comes from the heart and touches our hearts is eternal.

## Ariadne's Thread

As I finish this book, one of my friends, the writer Christiane Singer, has just died at the age of sixty-four from sudden, devastating cancer. She did not get the chance to live out her old age, an age that fascinated her all her life. Growing old was for her a blessing, for it was a process of moving toward an opening filled with light. "How many find the door that it opens?" she liked to wonder. But I have no doubt that the secrets of growing old, the "eleven beatitudes of old age,"[3] were revealed to her during the six months she was given to live by a young, cold-eyed doctor on September 1, 2006. She could have rebelled, or collapsed, but instead she greeted the ordeal unflinchingly.

"What has to be lived, I shall have to live," she wrote in a diary she kept from day to day, enabling us to share the ordeal she was going through and the gift that came with it.[4] Ground down, abraded, "sun-scorched" by suffering, she plunged into a kind of hell. "Get through it, noble girl, get through it," she repeated to herself, at the same time weeping over "the vulnerability of everything that is under the sun." So she got through it, with the aid of the Ariadne's thread that never left her since childhood: the thread of Wonder. "With its help, I shall emerge alive from the darkest of labyrinths." She got through, determined not to allow the illness to invade her: "A sickness is in me, but my work is not to be in the sickness myself."

What she had written earlier about old age held true for the brutally accelerated end of her life. "Why shouldn't I trust in my last 'incarnation,' the one which, in my own eyes and others', will make me look like an old woman? Why shouldn't I give myself with the same faith, the same conviction, the same inextinguishable curiosity? And even if my body shrivels up, if my limbs knot and stiffen, was the world's only beauty really in my bedroom mirror? Come now! Surely many other tangible wonders will remain outside of me, in everything that prolongs and continues my life, surrounds and multiplies me?"[5]

And, she says, she saw what she wanted to see. "When there is nothing left" — and she knows what she is talking about, for she experienced this extreme stripping-away process — "really nothing left, there isn't death and emptiness, as one might fear, not at all. I swear to you, there is nothing left but Love."[6]

A month before her death, I went to see her in Austria, to say good-bye. As I entered her room, I was struck by the way that her frail, terribly thin body and her face, hollow-cheeked with pain, contrasted with the peace that emanated from her, and with the vitality of her gaze and her smile. Christiane knew she was going to die. "I would so have loved to live longer, to grow old, to go on cradling the world," she told me.

"Cradling the world": that expression remains engraved in the depths of my heart. I promised myself then that I would spend my old age "cradling the world," and doing so while thinking of Christiane, who did not have that opportunity.

This is the great lesson that we can learn from Christiane, from Sister Emmanuelle, from Stéphane Hessel, and from so many others around us: when we no longer want anything, when we no longer expect anything, and when we leave everything up to Life, it is not bitterness or despair that dwells within us but a new feeling of unexpected freedom and a huge, immense tenderness.

One question haunted her, a question that also haunted me as I wrote this book: "How can we infect each other with fervor and life?"

On my return from Vienna, I discovered a note written by Jacques Decour at a time when he must surely have had a premonition of his end. Decour, a novelist and a professor of German, enlisted in the Intellectual Resistance during World War II. He fought keenly against the spirit of collaboration, and defended humanism against obscurantism. A founder — with Jean Paulhan — of the underground newspaper *Les Lettres françaises* in 1942, he was shot by the Nazis at Mont-Valérien at the age of thirty-two. As he awaited his execution in prison, he wrote a very touching letter to his family.

Now each of us is preparing to die. . . . We are preparing, thinking about what is to come, about what is going to kill us without our being able to do anything to defend ourselves. . . . This is truly the moment for us to remember love. Did we love enough? Did we spend hours a day marveling at other people, being happy together, feeling the value of contact, the weight and the worth of hands, eyes, bodies? Do we yet really know how to devote ourselves to tenderness? Before we pass away in the trembling of an earth without hope, it is time to become, entirely and definitely, love, tenderness, and friendship, because there is nothing else. We must swear to think of nothing anymore but loving, loving, opening our souls and our hands, looking with our best eyes, clasping what we love tightly to ourselves, walking free from anxiety, and radiant with affection.[7]

# ACKNOWLEDGMENTS

I should like to express my sincere thanks to Sister Emmanuelle (†) and Stéphane Hessel; to Arnaud Desjardins, Patrick Dewavrin, Robert Dilts, Olivier de Ladoucette, Yvonne Johannot, Robert Misrahi, Charles Salzmann (†), Christiane Singer (†), Annick de Souzenelle, Christopher Thiery, Jean-Pierre Van Rillaer, Bertrand Vergely, Aude Zeller; to all those who gave me their testimonies but who wished to remain anonymous; to Henry Rosenbloom, Liz Gough, and Amber Qureshi for their invaluable help in reaching readers across all seas; and to Nicole Lattes, Antoine Audouard, Susanna Lea, Laura Mamelok, and Kerry Glencorse for their confidence in me and their unfailing support.

# NOTES

*Please note that where the titles of French publications are followed by English titles in brackets, these are translations only and do not represent English editions.*

## I Write for My Generation

1. Abbé Pierre was the founder, in 1949, of the Emmaus movement, which was designed to help the poor and the homeless. He has remained a popular figure in France throughout the years, and his death in 2007 was a blow to many.

2. Paul-Laurent Assoun, Jean-Denis Bredin, and Marie de Hennezel, *Comment accepter de vieillir?* [How Should We Accept Growing Old?] (Ivrysur-Seine: Éditions de l'Atelier, 2003). (This book is based on the discussion.)

3. In his book *Rester jeune, c'est dans la tête* [Staying Young Is All in the Mind] (Paris: Odile Jacob, 2005), Olivier de

Ladoucette quotes a study conducted by the IPSEN foundation, which involved 910 centenarians. Two of the centenarians' psychological characteristics seemed decisive to the researchers: resilience (i.e., the ability to bear adverse life events and to find within oneself the resources needed to resist and to bounce back) and *conation* (the idea of intentional effort and energy focused toward the accomplishment of tasks).

4. Henry Greenberg, Susan U. Raymond, and Stephen R. Leeder, "Cardiovascular Disease and Global Health: Threat and Opportunity," *Health Affairs* web exclusive, January 25, 2005, http://content.health affairs.org/cgi/reprint/hlthaff.w5.31v1.pdf.

## When the Fear of Growing Old Assails You

1. Ram Dass, *Still Here: Embracing Aging, Changing, and Dying* (New York: Riverhead Books, 2000).
2. Speaking before the French parliamentary commission on accompanying individuals at the end of their lives.
3. Joël de Rosnay, Jean-Louis Servan-Schreiber, François de Closets, and Dominique Simonnet, *Une vie en plus* [Another Life] (Paris: Le Seuil, 2005).

4. Mitch Albom, *Tuesdays with Morrie* (London: Little, Brown, 1998).

## The Worst Is Not Inevitable

1. An article by Claire Gatinois in *Le Monde,* May 25, 2007, states that 84 percent of those aged sixty to seventy-nine have no financial problems. They are "a source of well-being in economic as well as cultural terms." The contribution of people over sixty years of age to the French economy is estimated at 7.5 billion euros per year.

## The Golden Age of Senior Citizens

1. *Paris Match,* August 10–16, 2006.
2. As the old saying goes: An apple a day keeps the doctor away.
3. *Une vie en plus.*
4. Ibid.
5. Ibid.

## Changing the Way We See

1. Armelle Canitrot, *La Croix* [The Cross], October 16, 2006. In this special report that was devoted to the image of old age, Armelle Canitrot wondered about the fact that "France is hiding her age." Taking note of newspapers' reticence to publish photos of very old people, she wrote: "An extraterrestrial whose only image of

French society was that provided by its media — press, television, advertisements, cinema — would unhesitatingly conclude that in France, no individual gets past the age of seventy. And yet today, one person in ten is aged over seventy-five!"

2. The other day, I cut out an advertisement from a weekly magazine aimed at senior citizens. It made me smile: the woman who was supposed to be using incontinence protection looked as if she had just celebrated her thirtieth birthday.

3. At the fifth meeting of the Eisai Foundation, April 5, 2007.

4. Michel Bony, *Il n'y a que toi et les oiseaux* [Just You and the Birds] (Paris: Ramsay, 1998).

5. Jean Théfaine, *Ouest-France* [West-France], August 22–23, 1998.

6. *Il n'y a que toi et les oiseaux.*

7. *L'Arène de France* was a French current-affairs talk show on which contentious questions were debated. Members of the public would vote before and after the debate, in order to reassess their views.

## Answering Fears About Old Age

1. Michelle Joyaux's organization, Grands-Parrains et Petits-Filleuls (Great-godparents and Grand-godchildren),

enables French children without grandparents to establish an affectionate relationship with adults who wish to act as honorary grandfathers and grandmothers to them.

2. Philippe Bas, minister for family affairs, 2005–2007.

3. In the suburbs of Dijon, seventy-six social apartments are available to people of different ages. In order to facilitate integration, everyone was asked to sign the "Hello, Neighbor" charter. The goal was to eliminate anonymity and to help everyone get to know and respect one another.

4. Laura Huxley's Project Caressing.

5. Benoîte Groult, *La touche étoile* [The Star Key] (Paris: Albin Michel, 2006).

6. Fondation Nationale de Gérontologie (National Gerontology Foundation), *C'était hier et c'est demain: lettres d'anciens jeunes à de futurs vieux* [It Was Yesterday and It Is Tomorrow: Letters from the Formerly Young to the Soon to Be Old] (Paris: Taillandier, March 2005).

7. Created by the Marie Gendron Association, Le Baluchon.

8. From an unattributed article in *La Croix*, April 29, 2005.

9. Ibid.

10. Ibid.

11. *Still Here: Embracing Aging, Changing, and Dying.*

12. Claudine Attias-Donfut, Boris Cyrulnic, Étienne Klein, and Robert Misrahi, *Penser le temps pour lire la vieillesse* [Thoughts on the Nature of Time, to Better Understand Aging] (Paris: Fondation Eisai/PUF, 2006).

13. *Tuesdays with Morrie.*

14. Ibid.

15. Danielle Thiébaud, *Le cahier de Marie* [Marie's Diary] (Laval: Siloë, 2004).

16. Ibid.

17. Ibid.

18. Ibid.

19. Ibid.

20. Ibid.

21. Laurence Serfaty, *Alzheimer jusqu'au bout de la vie* [Alzheimer's to the End of Life], Altomédia Productions, 2006.

22. Christian Bobin, *La présence pure* [Pure Presence] (Cognac: Éditions Le Temps qu'il fait, 1999).

23. Jean Maisondieu, *Le crépuscule de la raison* [The Twilight of Reason] (Montrouge: Éditions Bayard, 2001).

24. Aude Zeller, *À l'épreuve de la vieillesse* [Into the Breach of Old Age] (Paris: Desclée de Brouwer, 2003).

25. Ibid.

26. Ibid.

27. Ibid.

28. One such program is the IFR (Institut de Formation et de Recherche) (Institute of Training and Research), which trains individuals in humanistic approaches to care: 4 Petite Rue des Feuillants, 69001 Lyon, France; ifrhus@free.fr.

29. Florence Deguen, *Aujourd'hui* [Today], September 5, 2007.

## Encounters with Remarkable Elderly People

1. *"Dix témoignages de seniors magnifiques"* [Ten Testimonies by Magnificent Senior Citizens], *Nouvelles Clés* [New Keys], no. 51 (Autumn 2006). Based on extracts from Liliane Delawasse and Frédéric Delpêch, *Passionément Vieux* [Passionately Old] (Paris: Éditions Anne Carrière, 2005).

2. Robert Laffont passed away on May 19, 2010, at the age of ninety-three.

3. Sister Emmanuelle passed away on October 20, 2008, at the age of ninety-nine.

4. Sister Emmanuelle, *Vivre, à quoi ça sert?* [Life, What's the Point?] (Paris: J'ai Lu, 2005).

5. Ibid.

6. Ibid.

7. "But in the eye of the aged, one can see light," *Les contemplations* (Paris: Éditions Flammarion, 1999).

8. Stéphane Hessel, *Ô ma mémoire, la poésie, ma nécessité* [O My Memory, Poetry, My Necessity] (Paris: Le Seuil, 2006).

## Keys to a Happy Old Age

1. The allocation of 168 million euros was announced by the then minister for family affairs, Philippe Bas, on January 24, 2007.

2. Cicero, *De senectute* [On Old Age], or *Caton l'Ancien. De la vieillesse* [Cato Major, On Old Age], ed. and trans. Pierre Wuilleumier (Paris: Les Belles Lettres, 2002).

3. *Rester jeune, c'est dans la tête.*

4. Ibid.

5. Ibid.

6. *Une vie en plus.*

7. *Penser le temps pour lire la vieillesse.*

8. Robert Dilts, *Changing Beliefs with NLP* (Cupertino, CA: Meta Publications, 1990).

9. Ibid.

10. Becca R. Levy, Martin D. Slade, and Stanislav V. Kasl, "Longitudinal Benefit of Positive Self-Perceptions of Aging on

Functional Health," *The Journals of Gerontology Series B: Psychological Sciences and Social Sciences,* September 2002.

## Accepting Growing Old

1. Michel de M'Uzan, *Le travail du trépas. L'art et la mort* [The Task of Passing Away: Art and Death] (Paris: Éditions Gallimard, 1977).
2. Corinthians 4:16, La Bible de Jérusalem [The Jerusalem Bible] (Paris: Les Éditions du Cerf, 2003).
3. *Rester jeune, c'est dans la tête.*
4. Hermann Hesse, *Éloge de la vieillesse* [In Praise of Aging] (Paris: Le Livre de poche, 2000). The original German reference is *Mit der Reife wird man immer jünger — Betrachtungen und Gedichte über das Alter* [With Maturity You'll Always Be Younger — Reflections and Poems About Old Age] (Frankfurt: Suhrkamp Verlag, 2008).
5. Quoted by Christiane Singer in *Les âges de la vie* [The Ages of Life] (Paris: Albin Michel, 1990).
6. Karlfried Graf Dürckheim, *L'expérience de la transcendance* [The Experience of Transcendence] (Paris: Albin Michel, 1994). The original German reference is *Der Alltag als Übung. Vom Weg zur Verwandlung* [The Way of Transformation:

Daily Life as Spiritual Exercise] (Bern: Verlag Hans Huber, 2001).

7. Gérald Quitaud, *Vieillir ou grandir?* [To Grow Old or to Grow Up?] (Escalquens: Dangles, 2004).

8. This "darkness" is a concept proposed by Jung to explain the depth of unprocessed or repressed experiences.

9. *L'expérience de la transcendance.*

10. *La touche étoile.*

11. Jacqueline Kelen, *L'esprit de solitude* [The Spirit of Solitude] (Paris: Albin Michel, 2005).

12. Ibid.

13. Ibid.

14. Ibid.

## The Heart Does Not Grow Old

1. *Éloge de la vieillesse.*

2. "Bien sûr il y a des choses que je ne peux plus faire / mais d'autres que je peux et ne pouvais naguère / Tout a une fin, ma vie comme le reste/ Peut-être demain, ou au détour du chemin. / Pour l'heure il me semble que j'ai tout le temps / Pour aimer, pour bénir tous ceux qui m'ont rendu heureux, / Amour d'un instant ou amour pour longtemps / Je les garde au tréfonds de mon coeur apaisé. / Toujours ils me parlent de l'art d'aimer."

3. Évariste Boulay-Paty (1804–1864) was not yet sixty when he wrote those words, but we must remember that in that era the median age was only thirty-five.

4. Victor Hugo, *Correspondences,* quoted by Simone de Beauvoir in *La Vieillesse* [The Coming of Age] (Paris: Éditions Gallimard, 1970).

5. *Penser le temps pour lire la vieillesse.*

6. Ibid.

7. Ibid.

8. Ibid.

9. Ibid.

10. Claudine Badey-Rodriguez, *La vie en maison de retraite* [Life in a Retirement Home] (Paris: Albin Michel, 2003).

11. Maud Mannoni, *Le nommé et l'innomable. Le dernier mot de la vie* [The Named and the Unnameable: The Last Word of Life] (Paris: Denoël, 1991).

12. *Penser le temps pour lire la vieillesse.*

13. Baruch de Spinoza, *L'éthique* [Ethics] (Paris: Éditions Gallimard, 1994).

14. Ibid.

15. *Penser le temps pour lire la vieillesse.*

16. This meeting was held in January 2007. The full text of the meeting is available through the La Traversée Association, 12 Rue St. Sulpice, 75006, Paris.

17. Gilles Deleuze and Félix Guattari,

*Qu'est-ce que la philosophie?* [What Is Philosophy?] (Paris: Éditions Minuit, 1991).

18. *Penser le temps pour lire la vieillesse.*
19. Ibid.

## A Sensual Old Age

1. *Penser le temps pour lire la vieillesse.*
2. *Théma,* Arte, November 28, 2006. Featuring the German film *Plaisirs d'amour entre deux ages* [The Pleasure of Love Between Two Ages], directed by Silvie Banuls and Monika Kirschner, 2005.
3. Nancy Huston, *Une adoration* [An Adoration] (Arles: Actes Sud, 2003).
4. From the Arte program cited earlier.
5. Régine Lemoine-Danthois and Élizabeth Weissman, *Un âge nommé désir* [An Age Named Desire] (Paris: Albin Michel, 2006).
6. J. G. Bretschneider and N. L. McCoy, "Sexual Interest and Behavior in Healthy 80- to 102-year-olds," *Archives of Sexual Behavior,* April 1988.
7. Deirdre Fishel, *Still Doing It: The Intimate Lives of Women over 65,* Mind's Eye Productions, 2003.
8. *Rester jeune, c'est dans la tête.*
9. Alain Moreau, *Éloge de la vieillesse* [A

Eulogy to Old Age] (Paris: Bibliophane, 2006).

10. At the ESSIR (European Society for Sex and Impotence Research) Congress held in Rome in October 2001, Dr. Marc Ganem stated: "Apart from improving the state of health and notably the cardiorespiratory system, which ensures the oxygenation of the brain, sexual exercise could stimulate the synthesis of substances favorable to the development and upkeep of brain cells."

11. *Une vie en plus.*

12. *Rester jeune, c'est dans la tête.*

13. *Mieux vivre la vieillesse.*

14. Ibid.

15. Jolan Chang, *The Tao of Love and Sex* (Paris: Pocket, 2005).

16. Ibid.

17. Ibid.

18. Ibid.

19. Ibid.

20. Ibid.

21. Anaïs Nin, *The Journals of Anaïs Nin,* vol. 4 (Paris: Éditions Stock, 1972).

**The Fecundity of Time**

1. *Éloge de la vieillesse.*

2. Ibid.

3. Quoted by Roger Dadoun in *Manifeste*

*pour une vieillesse ardent* [Manifesto for a
Glowing Old Age] (Cadeilhan: Zuma,
2005).

4. Lorette Nobécourt, *En nous la vie des
morts* [Keeping the Dead Alive within Us]
(Paris: Grasset, 2006).

5. Quoted by Jérôme Pélissier in *La nuit,
tous les vieux sont gris* [At Night, the Old
Are Gray] (Paris: Bibliophane, 2003).

6. *Vieillir ou grandir?*

7. Yves Prigent, *L'éxperience dépressive: la
parole d'un psychiatre* [Experiencing Depression: A Psychiatrist's View] (Paris:
Desclée de Brouwer, 1994).

8. *L'expérience de la transcendance.*

9. *Éloge de la vieillesse.*

10. *L'expérience de la transcendance.*

11. Ibid.

12. *Une vie en plus.*

13. Ibid.

14. *La nuit, tous les vieux sont gris.*

15. Ibid.

16. Marcel Légaut, as quoted by Jérôme Pélissier.

17. *Éloge de la vieillesse.*

18. Ibid.

19. *Still Here: Embracing Aging, Changing,
and Dying.*

20. Ibid.

21. Gilles Farcet, preface in Ram Dass, *Vieillir en pleine conscience* [Conscious Aging] (Paris: Le Relié Poche, 2002).

22. *L'expérience de la transcendance.*

23. Ibid.

## The Last Joys of Old Age

1. Jean-Louis Chrétien, *La joie spacieuse* [Expansive Joy] (Paris: Éditions Minuit, 2007).

2. From an article by Robert Maggiori about *La joie spacieuse* by Jean-Louis Chrétien, in *Libération,* February 2007.

3. *La joie spacieuse.*

4. Ibid.

5. Albert Donval, *La Croix,* March 21, 2005.

6. From an interview documented by Nathalie Crom, Bruno Frappat, and Robert Migliorini in *La Croix,* February 26, 2003.

7. This expression is used by Christiane Singer in *Les âges de la vie.*

8. *Manifeste pour une vieillesse ardent.*

9. *La touche étoile.*

10. *Éloge de la vieillesse.*

## Knowing How to Die

1. Maurice Zundel, *À l'écoute du silence* [Listening to Silence] (Paris: Téqui, 1979).

2. *Tuesdays with Morrie.*

3. Marie-Louise von Franz, *Les rêves et la*

*mort* [Dreams and Death] (Paris: Fayard, 1955).

4. Dr. Édouard Ferrand reported in the recent study *"La mort à l'hôpital"* [Death in the Hospital], 2007, that three out of every four people die without any family or friends at their side.

5. *La touche étoile.*

6. Marie de Hennezel, *Nous ne nous sommes pas dit au revoir* [We Didn't Say Good-bye] (Paris: Robert Laffont, 2000).

7. Ibid.

## Conclusion

1. Quoted by Charles Salzmann in *Journal de l'île de Groix* [The île de Groix News] (Paris: Éditions Christian, 2004).

2. In the preface of my book *La mort intime* [Intimate Death] (Paris: Robert Laffont, 2001).

3. *Les âges de la vie.*

4. Christiane Singer, *Derniers fragments d'un long voyage* [Final Fragments of a Long Voyage] (Paris: Éditions Albin Michel, 2007).

5. *Les âges de la vie.*

6. *Derniers fragments d'un long voyage.*

7. From a letter attributed to Jacques Decour by the theologian Jean-Yves Leloup.

# INDEX

acceptance, 19, 29, 63, 152–53, 157–58, 225

*acedia* (sadness), 234

activities, 178–79

age:
  physiological, 45
  social or subjective, 45

ageism, 24, 32

age pyramid, 35

aging:
  denial of, 156
  working at, 257–58

"Aging Well" plan (France), 138–39

Alberte (parachute jumper), 212

Allen, Woody, 259

Alzheimer's disease:
  biogenesis explanation for, 105
  burden of, 35
  Carpe Diem home, 103
  film about, 103–4
  as taboo subject, 106, 109

Wiesel, Elie, 32
wine, red, 52
*Winged Migration* (Le peuple migrateur)
    (film), 236
wisdom, 159
  living in the now, 179–80
Wolinski, Georges, 50, 56–57
wonder, 235–38, 261, 263–67
World War II, Intellectual Resistance in,
    266

yin and yang, 203, 208
youth:
  emotional, 65
  of the heart, 61, 117, 171
  obsession with, 51, 62
  real youthfulness, 257–58
*yuimaru* (mutual cooperation), 21
*Yvonne* (92-year-old), 68–70, 152–55

Zeller, Aude, 106–8
Zundel, Maurice, 239–40

# ABOUT THE AUTHOR

**Marie de Hennezel** has spearheaded numerous national health initiatives in France over the last decade and regularly presents seminars on the art of aging well. She is the author of ten previous books, including the international bestseller *Intimate Death,* and is a recipient of the Legion of Honor Award.